THE IS MANAGEMENT AND BUSINESS CHANGE GUIDES

HOW TO MANAGE BUSINESS CHANGE

The IS Management and Business Change Guides

HOW TO MANAGE

Business

Change

FORMAT
PUBLISHING

Published by
Format Publishing Limited
9-10 Redwell Street
Norwich
Norfolk NR2 4SN
United Kingdom

General enquiries/telephone orders: **01603 766544**
Fax orders: **01603 761491**
Email: **sales@formatpublishing.co.uk**
Online ordering: **www.formatpublishing.co.uk**

Edited, designed and typeset by **Format Information Design**

Published for the Office of Government Commerce
under licence from the Controller of Her Majesty's Stationery Office.

First published 2001
ISBN 1903091101

For further information about this and other OGC products, please contact:
OGC Service Desk
Rosebery Court
St Andrews Business Park
Norwich NR7 0HS

Telephone: 0845 000 4999
Email: info@ogc.gsi.gov.uk
Website: www.ogc.gov.uk

Printed in the United Kingdom for Format Publishing

Contents

Executive summary

Change is a constant in today's business world. Effective management of change will help an organisation move towards its strategic goals by confronting key issues at an early stage and adopting a structured approach to making change happen.

A clear idea of what constitutes success, a realistic assessment of the organisation's capability to change, and detailed plans for how the change will be achieved are all vital to the change process. Without them, there is a danger that new systems or hierarchies will be created that fail to deliver any real benefits, or that deliver the wrong kinds of benefit. Even worse, the change effort may actively waste resources and make it necessary to return to the starting point.

The process of change

Change can be viewed as a cyclical process, with issues that need to be dealt with at each stage. These issues include why there is a need for change, where the organisation is now and where it wants to be, what needs to be changed, how to approach and implement change, and finally a review of the outcome. The lessons learned may in turn give rise to another cycle of change.

The drivers (reasons) for change in an organisation will influence the approach to change. Drivers may be external – for example, meeting the demands of public sector policy or customer service requirements, responding to market pressure or adapting to new technology – or internal, such as increased productivity, reducing costs, becoming more effective, quality assessment, developing human resources and IT issues. Change, therefore, may be voluntarily undertaken in order to realise specific benefits, or be forced upon an organisation by the business environment.

Examining the key issues facing your organisation will also help identify drivers for change. These challenges may be perceived as either problems or opportunities and may be business, technical, political or cultural in nature.

Planning the process

An organisation will greatly increase its chances of success if it plans change carefully. Any change initiative should support an organisation's strategic objectives. It is vital to formulate a clearly stated, realistic change goal that is easy to measure. You should avoid relative or unmeasurable goals that give a direction but no destination because they may result in an open-ended, unfocused change effort.

Similarly, without an idea of where the organisation currently stands there is no way of measuring the potential benefits of change. Asking the question 'Where are we now?' will help to define the starting point for the change process.

Defining the scope of the change will identify the implications of the change on the organisation and its environment, on strategy, structure, management processes, individuals and roles, and technology. There may, for example, be unintended changes or 'knock-on effects' that could destabilise the whole change effort. Scoping is important for anticipating difficulties before they arise, and assessing the value of breaking change down into achievable modules.

Organisational complexity

The context for any change is the close relationship between the pressures of the external business environment and an organisation's management, business processes, people, information and technology. Change can affect many different aspects of an organisation – service delivery, business processes, people systems, structures and facilities and technologies. IT in particular needs strategic management, because of its close integration with the business and its operations.

A central issue for managing change is recognising organisational complexity. Any attempt to implement a change in one area may have consequences elsewhere. For example, the introduction of new customer-oriented services may create problems for staffing (human resource development), but generate opportunities for reduced overheads (productivity and efficiency). It is also likely that at any given time there will be more than one change process going on in an organisation and these will need to be prioritised to avoid conflicting priorities with finite resources.

Complexity can also extend beyond the organisation, to key suppliers, partners, and other related organisations. This inter-organisational complexity makes a structured approach to change even more important.

'People' issues

The 'soft' issues involved in changing cultural aspects of the organisation, as well as infrastructures and hierarchies, should not be neglected. The attitudes and behaviours of those who make up the organisation can undermine a change initiative. The cultural drivers for stability, inertia and resistance within an organisation's culture must be tackled through continuous communication and involvement. Motivation and enthusiasm must be actively fostered throughout the change process through two-way communication, involvement and persuasion.

Stakeholders

In this context, a stakeholder is any body or person who will be affected by the proposed change. Stakeholders may include other organisations, political bodies, customers, staff, or the general public. A vital component of the change process is to identify stakeholders and ensure that they are involved in, and benefit from, the change.

The IT context

Most organisations depend on IT to manage their business information; increasingly they are deploying IT to deliver services to their customers. Failure to give adequate consideration to IT may lead to it becoming an inhibitor of change. Change may affect an organisation's IT infrastructure and provision must be made for current requirements and for the future. IT service providers should be major stakeholders in the change process. There should also be access to expert advice, particularly on the advantages and disadvantages of centrally co-ordinating IT and planning an e-business change.

The change owner

To have the best chance of success, a planned change needs to be managed and owned by a nominated individual with the necessary authority in the organisation to address the cultural and political obstacles to change. This individual is the 'change owner', who ensures that the change process is focused, throughout its lifecycle, on delivering its objectives and the projected benefits, and acts as a unitary point of contact with whom the change is identified.

Implementing change

It is important for the organisation's management to show commitment and leadership in order to give the change credibility. The way in which change is put into practice depends largely on the scale of the change. Some changes may be suitable for a transformational or 'big bang' approach, while others will require a more cautious approach of gradual steps, either through incremental change or modular change. The transitional stage may require interim arrangements to be put in place.

Adequate communication with staff is crucial, to 'unfreeze' existing attitudes and beliefs and to encourage receptivity to change by addressing concerns, offering training and support, and reinforcing key messages. During the transition phase, the benefits of change must be visible and communicated to staff, customers and stakeholders. Once change is complete the organisation must be 'refrozen' in its new form; the change must be assimilated into the organisational culture.

Pilot and demonstration projects are valuable at the implementation stage, because they can be used to confront varying expectations and uncertainties about the outcome or value of change.

Cultural resistance to change can come from many sources: fear of the unknown, concern over changes to organisational culture, lack of confidence in the change management, changes in power relationships and corporate memory of past change initiatives. Making trade-offs, creating group prestige, retaining links with the past, retaining familiar practices and forming coalitions are all techniques for overcoming resistance.

Realising the benefits

Finally, it is necessary to review the change to assess its success; to identify and manage the benefits from it. The benefits of change may be direct or indirect, financial or intangible. Some may depend on other benefits to be realised. Early, highly visible benefits – 'quick wins' – will be desirable when the change is spread over a long period.

Change often opens up opportunities for further improvements; regular reviews should assess the potential for increasing the benefits from investment in change.

Introduction

No organisation stands still. In fact, in today's business environment, change has become a constant. Changes in the business environment, new customer demands, advances in technology, and changing expectations of staff are just a few of the pressures that force continuing change on every organisation. The demands of the information age have made rapid, efficient change and adaptation more of a necessity than ever before.

This publication replaces the earlier IS Management Guide *Managing Change,* which explained concepts about change and aimed to increase understanding of those concepts. It should form a useful introduction to the process of change and the issues that must be considered as you move through it, with particular emphasis on the 'soft' or 'people' issues that can make or break a change programme. It forms an introduction to more specific, practical guidance such as that contained in the other publications in this series and in particular the complementary guide *Managing Successful Programmes.*

Technology has become an essential factor in organisational change. This publication includes sections dealing specifically with the role that Information Technology (IT) can play in change.

1.1 The need to manage change

The four main reasons why change must be managed can be stated very simply.

- Planned changes must be managed in order to deliver benefits.

- Poorly managed change could be catastrophic for the organisation.

- Change can be complex.

- Organisational culture is a critical factor in change.

Planned changes must be managed

On the most basic level, the intended change must be managed because if nobody is responsible for a change, it is unlikely to take place. Although this sounds obvious, many proposed changes founder for want of a manager or champion to make them happen. It must be someone's job to manage a change, plan the necessary activities, obtain approval, assemble the resources, undertake the work and ensure that everyone plays their part. For a major change, a Programme Manager may be appointed with far-reaching powers and responsibilities; a single individual may be enough to carry out a minor change. But whatever the change management requirement, it must be met for the change to succeed.

Poorly managed change

The consequences of a poorly managed change could be catastrophic for the organisation. The wider the scope of the proposed change, the greater the potential for disaster. It is vital that the change initiative be managed efficiently from the very start. A clear idea of what constitutes success, a realistic assessment of the organisation's capability to change, and detailed plans for how the change will be achieved are all essential; none of them will happen by accident. Without them, there is a very real danger that new systems or hierarchies will be created that do not deliver any real benefits, failing to move the organisation towards its strategic goals. Another danger is that they deliver the wrong kinds of benefit, drawing the organisation towards other, unintended, destinies.

The worst case scenario is that the change not only delivers no benefits but actively wastes resources and makes it necessary to backtrack, removing systems and dismantling hierarchies, in order to return to the starting point. Proper change management will prevent these scenarios, if only by prompting those involved to ask the right questions at an early enough stage to halt the change initiative before significant investment is made.

Change can be complex

At a deeper level, the change to be managed can be complex, due to the systemic or 'holistic' nature of organisational change. As soon as the organisation moves beyond very simple changes, it needs to take account of a variety of interrelated factors which can make the management of change a complex requirement. The problem of organisational complexity is discussed in more detail later in this publication.

The most important point to recognise is the potential for difficulty and complexity inherent in making changes to your organisation, and not to underestimate the work involved. The process of change can be cyclic and its structure is flexible, but it should never become an unfocused, indefinite period of upheaval that is embarked on without direction, continued without focus or monitoring, and ended when those involved are unable to continue.

Organisational culture

Much of the management of change is a highly disciplined, rational process, involving careful planning, scheduling and resource allocation. But the 'soft' issues must also be taken into account. The importance of changing cultural aspects of the organisation, as well as infrastructures and hierarchies, should not be neglected. It is not enough to develop a new business model or organisational hierarchy on paper and wait for it to take effect. The attitudes and behaviours of those who make up the organisation have more than enough power to derail such a course of action. The forces of inertia and resistance within an organisation's culture must be tackled through communication and involvement; motivation and enthusiasm must be actively fostered. All this takes time and careful management.

1.2 Who should read this guide

This guide is intended for:

- business managers sponsoring change efforts in the organisation

- programme managers and change agents responsible for planning and implementing organisational change programmes

- IT delivery units within the organisation, and external IT service providers and partners, contributing to programmes of organisational change

- anyone who wishes to learn about managing organisational change.

This publication is intended as an overview of the issues that arise during the change process. It will form a useful introduction to business change and the foundation for further reading on the actual techniques that you can use to build a successful programme of change. For full descriptions of the management processes and control approach that should be used when managing a change programme, please see the complementary guide *Managing Successful Programmes*.

1.3 Kinds of change

There are many kinds of change, and many reasons why change takes place. Identifying the kind of change you are facing is an important first step along the process of change.

Planned and unplanned

Some changes are planned. The need for them is foreseen and they are undertaken voluntarily by the organisation in order to reach planned objectives or realise specific benefits. Planned changes include:

- improving efficiency: doing what you do more quickly, or doing more of it in the same time

- improving effectiveness: doing what you do better, preferably without a trade-off in terms of cost or time

- improving economy: spending less money for the same results

- moving into new areas of business: offering new services, or the same services in a radically new way (online rather than face-to-face, for example)

- moving out of existing areas of activity

- providing better services

- restructuring following the merging or separating of two organisational units, or the acquisition of one company by another.

Other changes are unplanned. These changes have not been foreseen and are undertaken whether the organisation wants them or not. Examples of unplanned changes include:

- in the public sector, responding to new policy requirements

- correcting a serious, possibly worsening problem that has been neglected, ignored or not fully appreciated until now

- responding to adverse business conditions – for example, dealing with new competition or erosion of market share by uncontrollable forces

- utilising a new, rapidly developing technology that cannot be ignored by the organisation.

Another type of unplanned change is that of recovering from a change effort that has failed: undoing what has recently been changed and restoring it to its previous state, and taking out unwanted systems.

The kind of change your organisation is facing will directly affect the manner in which it is approached. For example, it would not be helpful to adopt a cautious, step-by-step approach to a situation in which your organisation is losing money every day – even if you engineer a perfect solution, it might come too late. Conversely, if the business is healthy it would be foolish to move into radically new areas of business without careful planning, looking at the risks involved and possibly carrying out some pilot studies. Choosing the right approach for your situation is a major factor in successful change and, while this guide provides many perspectives on change, the way you deploy them will depend on your own situation.

Bounded and unbounded   Some changes are more problematic than others. Bounded changes are finite in scope. They are relatively simple to manage and it is easy to say when they have been completed. Unbounded changes have no such limits and are correspondingly difficult to manage.

Another way to express this distinction, proposed by Ackoff, is in terms of 'difficulties' and 'messes'. Where the scope of the change is strictly limited, and the change can be implemented through standard procedures and without wider repercussions, the situation can be described as a 'difficulty'. Difficulties require management and effort to resolve, but they are relatively simple to manage. Where the scope of change includes 'large and complex sets of interacting problems', the situation can be described as a 'mess'.

Difficulties are essentially bounded in scope, and amenable to routine solutions. Messes are essentially unbounded – it is not easy to say exactly where to 'draw the line' and exclude certain factors from consideration.

The differences between difficulties and messes, as applied to the management of change, are summarised in Table 1. You may find that you recognise characteristics of 'messy' changes you have lived through or observed.

It is important to know whether you are facing a difficulty or a mess. If you are faced with a mess, and assume that it is only a difficulty, the chances of success will be severely reduced. A mismanaged change process may turn difficulties into messes, and this should never be allowed to happen.

Table 1
Difficulties and messes

The differences between difficulties (bounded in scope and relatively easy to manage) and messes (unbounded in scope and more problematic to manage)

Difficulties	Messes
Essentially bounded in scope	Essentially unbounded in scope
Limited number of people involved; easy to identify all the people involved	Not easy to identify all the people involved
Objectives of the change effort are clear and well understood	Objectives of the change effort are unclear; there is no agreement on objectives amongst the parties involved
Priorities for the change are clear	There is uncertainty over priorities for the change
Nature of the problem is clear and so is what needs to be changed	Nature of the problem is not clear; there is disagreement over what the problem is and what needs to be changed
Relevant solutions are easily identified	Not clear what would constitute a 'solution'
The change can be considered largely in isolation from its environment	The change must be considered in the context of its environment
All relevant information is known or accessible	Not clear what information is relevant to the situation; or information is unreliable, or hard to find
Change effort is limited in timescale, or timescale is known	Longer timescale required for change effort, or timescale not easy to define
Factors are quantifiable	Factors are largely subjective

1.4 Areas for change

Change can affect many different aspects of an organisation. Some examples are given below:

- **service delivery**: the development of new types of services to customers (including the general public), possibly based on new technologies and communications facilities; the implementation of service delivery shared with other bodies

- **business processes**: re-engineering of business processes, possibly to exploit the potential of IT, including the transfer of processes to external partners or other public sector bodies

- **people systems**: changes in roles, responsibilities and working relationships; requirements for reskilling based on new technologies

- **structures and facilities**: establishment of new organisations, agencies and partnerships

- **technologies**: the implementation of new IT infrastructures to support internal and external communications and information sharing.

1.5 The IT context

The pace of change in information technology means that it is in a constant state of flux; each generation of business applications and IT infrastructure is improved upon or even superseded by the next wave of developments at ever-shortening intervals. With each stage of technological advance, organisations have become increasingly dependent on their IT facilities, and IT has become more closely integrated with the business and its operations. Managing the planning and development of the IT on which the organisation depends has become a critical part of the process of managing organisational change. It must be managed strategically.

Strategic management of IT in the organisation involves the interrelated activities of:

- **strategy**: developing and maintaining the information systems strategy for the organisation

- **acquisition**: acquiring and implementing the IT facilities needed to realise the strategy

- **delivery**: delivering IT-based services within and outside the organisation to meet business and administrative objectives, as set out in the organisation's IT strategy.

All these activities are managed and controlled to ensure that the desired organisational performance is achieved at management and operational levels. This may be made more complex when the provision, implementation and delivery are dependent on third parties outside the organisation.

1.6 Research for this guide

The research for this guidance was drawn from lessons learned in OGC's customer base, together with good practice being adopted internationally. It builds on earlier studies and guidance published by OGC on the management of change, and complements OGC's advice and guidance on Programme Management. The contributions of the many public and private sector participants in the development of this guidance are acknowledged with thanks.

2.1 Overview of the change process

The change process is a framework for considering, analysing and managing the issues around change. It is not a prescriptive, detailed sequence of activities, but can be tailored to circumstances. Every change process will be different; you should aim to use this guidance creatively and flexibly.

Throughout the text you will find references to other OGC guidance that you may find useful if you want to read further on related subjects such as managing risk. The OGC publication *Managing Successful Programmes* will be of particular interest, since it describes the processes and techniques that make planning and executing a large-scale programme of change much easier.

Figure 1
The process of change

The process of change, from the initial reasons why change should happen to review, and the questions that arise along the way

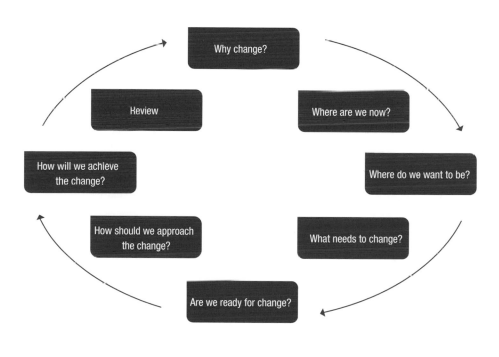

Figure 1 shows the change process as a cycle and the questions that arise along the way. The first question is 'why change?'; this leads to consideration of where the organisation is and what outcomes are desired, the planning and implementation of a change effort, and finally a review of the outcome. The results of the review, combined with the impact of other changes in the organisation and external developments, will eventually give rise to another cycle of change. In addition, it is likely that at any given time there will be more than one change process going on in an organisation.

After a major change effort, everyone in the organisation will probably be hoping for a period of stability. But periods of 'steady state' are unlikely to last long. In the public sector, new initiatives show no sign of slackening, and the pressure of competition is ever-present for all organisations. For both public and private sectors, developments in IT are constantly suggesting new options for improvements in internal administration and service delivery.

The stages in the process of change will involve iteration and backtracking, negotiation and experimentation. There will not always be a clear division between the different phases of activity, and some activities will have to be done out of sequence.

2.2 Programmes and projects

In the context of this publication and related guidance, the terms 'programme management' and 'project management' have distinct, specific meanings. The brief overviews below clarify the differences between them.

The guidance in this publication should be useful no matter what kind of change is in prospect. It provides an overview of all the issues involved and the questions that need to be answered, whether you are managing a single project, a group of projects, or a major programme of change. It is hoped that it will form the entry point for those beginning to read about managing change.

For practical, step-by-step guidance on the processes and techniques for managing projects and programmes, you will need to consult complementary and related guidance. Your organisation will greatly increase its chances of success and reduced risk if it follows structured approaches to the management of programmes of change and the projects that make up those programmes.

Programme management

A programme is a group of projects that are managed together to achieve a higher-level, strategic aim. It has a vision of the 'end-state' towards which it will move the organisation, but no clearly defined path to get there.

Programme management is the co-ordinated management of a portfolio of projects that create change to achieve benefits of strategic importance. It is a broadly spread activity and is concerned with more broadly defined change objectives than project management. It provides the framework for implementing large-scale change where you need to implement several projects, each a change process in itself, to achieve it.

Programme management requires clear understanding of strategic business plans to ensure appropriate scoping and alignment of projects. It co-ordinates stakeholder needs and organisational policies with the direction and timeframes for delivery of the projects. It involves continuous re-assessment of the benefits achieved against the context of the business environment to ensure the programme and its projects remain aligned to achieving the strategic aims.

For full guidance on programme management, consult the complementary OGC volume *Managing Successful Programmes*.

Project management

A project has a definite start and finish point, with the aim of delivering a product, service or specific outcome. Benefits result from a project after its output has been delivered.

Project management is a structured management framework for planning and progressing projects to deliver new products and services. It requires clear definition of required outcomes to ensure focused delivery of appropriate products and services. It is best suited to objectives that are closely bounded and relatively certain.

Project management incorporates the business drivers/constraints of time, cost, quality and risk. It is typically used within a programme management framework to align groups of projects against business objectives.

PRINCE 2 is a widely accepted standard for the management of projects. There are many publications on PRINCE 2, including *Managing Successful Projects with PRINCE 2*.

2.3 Factors for success

Everyone has lived through attempts to introduce changes in their organisation, some more successful than others. Some far-reaching changes have been implemented successfully. Other apparently minor changes have resulted in unintended consequences and disruption going far beyond the expectations of the unfortunate person responsible for managing the change activity. What distinguishes the successes from the failures?

There is no single prescription for the successful management of organisational change; organisations and their cultures, and the nature of change efforts, vary enormously. But there are certainly lessons to be learned from past attempts at organisational change, and from the experience of those involved, that are universally applicable. From these lessons have emerged two sets of requirements: corporate preconditions, which are the attributes of an organisation that is ready for successful change, and critical success factors, which are the attributes of a successful change process.

Corporate preconditions

For an organisation to be able to achieve successful outcomes from change, there must be a set of corporate preconditions in place. These preconditions relate to the way the organisation conducts all its programmes and projects. They are useful indicators of the organisation's ability to manage change and learn from experience. They are as follows:

- **business strategy**: there must be a clear direction set out in the business strategy, which is owned by all key stakeholders and informs all investment in business change

- **alignment to the strategy**: top management continually monitor and review investment in business change to ensure that it remains aligned with the business strategy as it evolves in response to changes in the business environment

- **roles and responsibilities understood**: unequivocal commitment from top management, partners and ministers/directors and a clear understanding of their continuing roles in achieving successful outcomes

- **skills and capabilities in place**: the organisation has access to the skills and capabilities it needs to achieve the desired outcomes from business change and is realistic about its abilities to manage complex change

- **organisational learning**: the organisation has defined, repeatable processes in place to learn from experience in managing change and to adopt better practices as a result of that experience, supported by appropriate training and development

- **a framework for managing risk**: the organisation has defined the roles, responsibilities and processes for managing risk across the organisation, with clearly defined routes for referral of risks to senior management.

Critical success factors

These are the attributes of successful change processes. Without them, a change effort is likely to fail. You will find fuller discussions of each critical success factor later in this publication.

- **definition**: a definition of the change to be made has been set out; those planning and leading the change have a clear understanding of its purpose and required outcome

- **management commitment**: senior management fully understand, and agree with, the reasons for the change and are committed to its success

- **recognising organisational complexity**: those in charge of the change fully understand the interrelated factors and issues that must be managed in order for the change to be successful

- **change owner**: a single figure has been nominated as the head of the change effort, in whom responsibility rests and to whom questions and problems are ultimately referred

- **the right people**: those who are tasked with making the change happen have the right skills, abilities and experience to manage all the issues – technical, organisational and political – that will arise

- **communication and involvement**: everyone who will be affected by the change is aware of their role, what the change will mean for them, and how the organisation and its business processes will be different after the change

- **staff development and support**: those who have to implement the change or who will be at the cutting edge of any new business processes are fully trained and supported in new areas

- **institutionalising change**: the change must be 'made to stick'; new ways of working must be adopted and seen to be an improvement; the change must be managed efficiently so that reverting to old methods does not become attractive or even inevitable.

This section considers the reasons for change and where change might take you. It is about answering two questions: 'why change?' and 'where do we want to be?'

3.1 Why change?

There are many possible reasons for change. The reason behind the change will influence what you do and how you approach the change.

You may already be clear about why your organisation needs to change, or even what needs to change. The areas in which you should concentrate your efforts during the change process will depend on what, in the broadest sense, is driving change in your organisation.

- If the reason for the change is clear, your change will be context driven.

- If what has to change is clear, your change will be content driven.

- If the goals or objectives are clear, your change will be outcome driven.

In a situation of **context driven change**, some aspect of the business or organisation needs improvement. There may be no clear desired outcome at this stage, and the content of the required change may be uncertain, but the reason for the change is clear. Reorganisations and process re-engineering are examples of this type of change.

Content driven change arises from the need to change some defined aspect of the business or organisation. The change may be prompted by, for example, the need to replaced outdated computer systems. The content of the change is clear but the desired outcome may not be obvious and will need to be defined. Decisions will need to be taken about the objectives of the change and the change process to be adopted.

Outcome driven change means you may have a clear vision of the desired future state for the business or organisation, but do not necessarily know how to realise it. The desired outcome may be imposed from outside, as for the targets set for government departments for the shift to electronic service delivery.

The change may also be driven by two, or all, of these factors in combination; for example, it may be clear why change is necessary and what has to change, but the final goal may not yet have been clarified, or may be unknowable. Or it may be that the reasons for change are clear, and the final goal is evident, but what has to change to bring it about is not yet decided.

3.2 Drivers for change and stability

One way to analyse the reason for change is to consider it as the combined result of several drivers for change. Drivers for change are factors that push the organisation towards change.

A number of drivers for change may be acting on the organisation. There will almost certainly be drivers for stability as well – drivers that resist change, that drive the organisation to stand still. Every organisation is under constant pressure to react to drivers for change and stability, which come from within and outside the organisation, and co-exist in a state of dynamic tension. Your organisation has to be aware of, and make efforts to deal with, the drivers that act upon it.

Drivers for change vary in nature and urgency, from external pressures such as changes in policy for public sector organisations to the need to rethink the way a company utilises its information resources. Understanding them will help in planning a change, and in assessing the wider impact of proposed changes. A change affecting any one of the drivers may conflict with, or may support, the pressures associated with the other drivers.

Drivers for stability are the internal pressures tending towards the maintenance of stability and equilibrium – the 'inertia' of an organisation. They may include the preservation of the status quo and maintenance of tradition, and also the existence of monitoring and regulation mechanisms that support the exercise of control. Every organisation has a strong tendency to remain as it is; this characteristic is true of many aspects of the organisation. Infrastructure is costly to change; hierarchies and power structures evolve slowly (if at all); people tend not to change their ways of working spontaneously, or may resist such change. Because of their nature – cultural rather than official, extant rather than nascent – drivers for stability can be difficult to define, or even to perceive from within the organisation. But their hold on the organisation must be taken into account when planning a change. Those outside the organisation, or who have joined recently, may be best placed to discern the inertia of an organisation. Those who have been inside it for a long time may be less so; bear in mind that they may include the senior management whose approval and commitment will be vital to the change.

A more practical definition of a driver for change is 'a view held by senior management as to what is important in the business, such that changes must occur in a given timescale'. Gaining commitment to the change will be simpler if a direct linkage can be made between the driver(s) and the objectives of the change; for example: 'changes in customer expectations mean that we must offer services online in order to retain a share of our target market'.

A key message is that if due attention is not paid to the underlying drivers of change, no amount of project management or input of resources will make the change programme a success.

External drivers

External drivers for change will vary widely depending on the nature of the organisation. Some examples are listed below (some are more applicable to public sector organisations):

- the pressures of public sector policy, other mandatory requirement, or the demands of *Modernising Government*

- the need to provide better services for customers

- market pressure from competitors

- pressures for improved effectiveness

- technological developments that make new services possible or suggest improvements to existing systems.

Internal drivers

Some possible internal drivers for change and stability are listed below. Again, some are particularly relevant to the public sector:

- **efficiency**: pressures for improved management of performance and the need to become more productive

- **economy**: the need to respond to pressures on resources, to reduce overheads (including time overheads), and to show real savings in day-to-day operations

- **effectiveness**: the need to do things better, and improve services to customers

- **quality**: the requirement for continuous improvement, often assessed through benchmarking comparisons with other organisations

- **human resource development**: pressures to maintain morale and cohesion, to motivate and develop staff, and treat them fairly; pressures for empowerment of staff

- **IT issues**: the need to update the IT infrastructure, to rethink how information is managed, or to enable new ways of working.

Backward mapping –
drivers from the cutting edge

Most of the guidance in this publication is built on the assumption of change being initiated by senior management. This assumes that there are clear lines of communication (both lateral and hierarchical) and control in the organisation, through which people are made aware of the need for change.

It is also important that communication be two-way; it must be more than the imposition of knowledge or ideas from above. In many organisations, the 'top-down' approach to change neglects the expertise and awareness at lower levels in the organisation. Staff at the cutting edge of service delivery will accumulate a vast amount of information on what needs to be remedied, and what might be constructively changed. The benefits of explicitly drawing on this pool of knowledge will be particularly valuable where, for example:

- the hierarchy, policies or culture of the organisation inhibit the flow of information from lower levels

- policy making and operational activities are handled by discrete divisions within the organisation

- operations are largely determined by bureaucratic rules and procedures that are difficult to change.

The backward mapping approach recognises that many initiatives for change will arise from the lowest level of implementation in the organisation, based on the experience of staff directly involved in service delivery. These staff will be able to suggest changes in behaviours and organisational activities that will reduce or eliminate problems in service delivery; the suggestions can be translated into the need for changes in policies at higher levels.

Based on these suggestions, management and planners can formulate objectives and policies for changes in the organisation that will produce the desirable changes in behaviours and activities.

This enables the planners to assess the impact of the proposed objectives and policies on the higher levels of the organisation or agencies. They identify the ability of each unit concerned to support the desired changes in behaviour, and the necessary changes in resources and procedures that will be required.

The final stage in the exercise is to formulate policies and strategies that will define the procedures and direct resources to the relevant units in the organisation where they will have most impact.

Backward mapping is suggested as a complementary approach to 'top-down' or forward mapping, not a replacement for it. The relevance and implications of backward mapping should be borne in mind in the early stages of a management of change programme. Otherwise, the strategies that are developed will be less likely to alter the behaviours and activities at the level of contact with the public, where the performance of the organisation is most visible.

Backward mapping may require a cultural shift towards openness. Staff may be very unfamiliar or uneasy with direct, two-way communication; indeed, many may never have experienced it. They will need to feel confident that their input will be valued and taken on board. If management pay lip service to 'listening' and then drive through what was originally envisaged anyway, staff will be demoralised.

Staff may also worry that speaking out may be held against them in some way; to hear the most honest feedback you will need to instil in them the confidence that this will not happen. This feeling may be intensified if, for whatever reason, you are not in a position to respond to the concerns raised; staff may then feel they have said things that management did not want to hear.

Force Field analysis

A useful technique to identify the forces acting on the organisation that will promote or inhibit change is Force Field analysis, developed by Lewin; it provides a way of identifying where effort will be required in assisting the change and overcoming resistance to it.

Figure 2
Force Field analysis

Forces acting from the left are pushing the organisation towards change, while those acting from the right resist change. If the resistant forces can be lessened, the organisation will move in the direction of the desired change

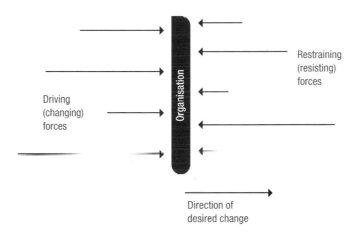

Figure 2 shows an organisation in a state of dynamic tension. There are forces at work, pushing in different directions, that have settled into a state of equilibrium and cancel each other out. If one or more driving forces in the situation can be strengthened, or one or more restraining forces weakened, then the situation will be shifted in the direction of the desired change.

The analysis should make some estimate of the 'strength' of each force – that is, the influence it has in the current situation and the difference that would be made by a change in that influence. Attention should be focused on the strongest forces, since addressing one or two of those could make all the difference in effecting the desired change.

It is important to describe the forces in terms that enable the necessary action to be identified; you need to be able to do something about strengthening or weakening the force as described. For example, if there is resistance to the introduction of an IT system because a previous attempt failed, the restraining force could be identified as 'concern of staff about the chances of success'. Attention can then be focused on weakening that force; for example, by finding ways to address staff concerns and demonstrating that the necessary lessons have been learned. It would not be much help to identify 'failure of previous implementation' as a restraining force, since there is nothing you can do about that now.

3.3 Identifying key issues

Another way to identify drivers for change is to look at the issues facing your organisation. Issues are challenges that must be addressed by the organisation; they may represent problems or opportunities. Successfully addressing a business issue will form a key success factor for the organisation's overall business strategy.

Almost all major change efforts are likely to include an IT element. For IT-related change the focus will be on issues that include an IT element, or for which IT developments will form part of the solution. The organisation's IT strategies will address these issues, through the identification of themes that will be pursued in the realisation of the strategies. Further details on the role of strategic themes for IT are given in the companion guide *How to manage Business and IT Strategies*.

The sources of issues facing the organisation, and examples of the related areas in which change may be required, can be categorised as:

- **business**
  - responding to customers
  - dealing with competition
  - new requirements for products and services
  - requirements for partnering and other new external relationships
  - new ways of doing business, such as self-assessment or electronic delivery
  - reorganisation to improve efficiency
- **technical**
  - application of IT to the business
  - exploitation of developments in the technological environment
  - management of information in the business
  - structure of tasks and processes in the organisation
  - facilities for communication within and outside the organisation
  - systems for management, monitoring and regulation

- **political**
  - decision processes
  - sources of power and influence in the organisation
  - definition of policy
  - relationships with the external environment
- **cultural**
  - organisational values
  - communication in the organisation
  - attitudes of stakeholders
  - competencies of staff
  - internal structures and relationships.

3.4 The context of change

Figure 3 shows the context of change. The business environment supplies external pressures on management to initiate change. Management, in the centre, must take account of four main factors in initiating and planning change: the organisation's business processes, people, information and technology.

The four factors shown on the diagram are all closely interlinked. A change in any one will affect the others, and no one factor has priority – in other words, no change effort should be just about technology or just about business. You must take account of all the factors when planning change. In particular, you should never fail to take full account of the impact that people will have on your proposed change.

3.5 Where do we want to be?

In trying to define the overall direction for the business, you may find it helpful formulate a change goal. Your change goal may be sweeping and transformational – for example, 'to combine operations with Organisation X, develop common business processes and provide fully integrated services within two years'. Or it may affect specific areas of business: 'to offer services x, y and z on an e-business basis within a year'.

Whatever your goal, and whatever its timescale, ensure that it is specifically worded. If you are going to establish a new operation, decide what 'established' means. If the goal is savings or revenue, decide how much is enough. If you want to streamline an operation, decide on its ideal new form.

Goals that are relative or hard to measure will not be helpful to you when reviewing the change process later on. They will give you a direction, but not a destination. As a result, you will find it hard to gauge the success of your change

Figure 3:
The context of change

The context of change, showing the inter-relationships of internal and external factors that will influence the change

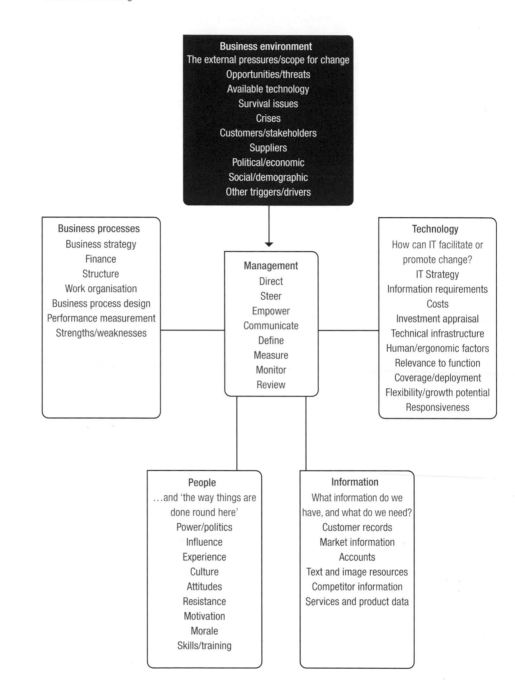

programme. Examples of relative goals would be 'to increase revenue' or 'to improve service delivery'. Examples of unmeasurable goals include 'to be the best provider of service x in the country', 'to lead the market in y' or 'to turn loss into profit in as short a time as possible'. While these goals obviously indicate a constructive desire to change the organisation for the better, trying to implement them may result in an open-ended, unfocused change effort – a 'mess' as described in the introduction.

Remember 'where we want to be' is your high-level goal, an ideal to aim for rather than your plans for the next few months. Make it challenging enough to arouse people's interest and enthusiasm – to create a sense of something new to be aimed for. If you already have a stated goal or goals, try to devise a new form of words even though your goals may not have changed a great deal.

Offset a sense of realism against the need for a challenge. If the desired goal could never be achieved with the resources you have (or will have) available, you are bound to fail. Keep it realistic as well as challenging. It may be helpful to think of it as a distillation of the sentiments that staff at all levels often have about the kind of organisation you could be, 'if only...'

The change goal should help to focus your thoughts on the change process. This is because it is immutable – unlike your expectations of the change process, which are likely to change as you progress into the stages of diagnosis and planning. The change goal can form the yardstick against which the results of the change process are measured. Throughout the change process and particularly during the final stages of review, when you look back on the process and gauge the benefits, it will serve as a useful reminder of the core purpose of the change and a means of gauging its success.

3.6 Evolution and revolution

The kind of change you consider will depend on whether your current situation differs from your goal by degree or by nature. If it differs by degree, your organisation needs to make evolutionary changes – to carry out its business better, faster or cheaper; do more of it; or offer more variations on it; or refine it in some other way. If the goal differs from the organisation's situation by nature, the change that is needed is radical, or revolutionary – new services, profound reorganisation, or some other major change of direction. It may also be that the change has been forced upon your organisation – an unplanned change.

The kind of change in prospect will have a profound effect on the scope of the change.

3.7 Strategic fit

You must ensure that the change is consistent with the overall direction of your organisation. There should be clear links between the business strategy, the organisation's strategic objectives and the proposed change to deliver those objectives; this is 'strategic fit'. For example, a key part of your business strategy might be to provide customers with better access to your services; a strategic objective supporting that strategy would be to reach 25% of your customers with online services within two years. In order to achieve that objective, there could be a proposed change involving development and enhancement of services that are particularly suitable for online delivery.

For each strategic objective, you would expect to identify change initiatives to deliver those objectives; without the change it would be impossible to achieve the objectives.

Conversely, if the change initiative would not deliver benefits that support those key objectives, you should not take it forward.

Taking stock

This chapter covers taking stock of the organisation and scoping the change process. The questions to be answered are 'where are we now?' and 'what needs to change?'

Defining the scope of the change does not mean specifying it in detail. There will still be some uncertainty about the desired outcomes, the paths to implementation, and detailed plans to bring the change about. For far-reaching or revolutionary changes, it is possible that there will not be complete agreement on objectives, or full understanding of the cause and effect chains involved. The emphasis should be on:

- defining the scope of the required change

- understanding the drivers and requirements for change, and the readiness, at a general level, of the organisation for change

- collecting and reconciling the views of the stakeholders in the situation

- ensuring that both business and IT interests have been adequately considered

- understanding the political and cultural aspects of the change

- generating commitment to the change

- obtaining a holistic view of the change situation and the relationships between the elements.

Some of these issues are discussed in the following chapter.

4.1 Where are we now?

Before you decide what will change, you must understand where you are starting from. On a simplistic level, if you 'subtract' where you are now from where you want to be, you will be left with what needs to change.

If extensive change programmes are in prospect, it may be helpful to produce a report on the current status of the organisation, or commission an unbiased survey from external consultants. Such a report could usefully describe the organisation's culture. This may help to dispel internal 'myths' about the organisation – both positive and negative – that might prejudice the change planning process.

The baseline and the 'do nothing' option

The baseline is the starting point from which the change process begins. The baseline is the state of your organisation at present; a 'snapshot' that encompasses procedures, structures and the business carried out by the organisation but makes no assumptions about the future.

When considering change, and assuming that the change is not being forced upon you, there is always the option to 'do nothing' – to continue operating as at present; the baseline option. Often appealing to organisations facing an uncertain future, the baseline option seems to offer a risk-free short- or medium-term strategy. It is particularly compelling for organisations that have already undergone major change, for whom plunging into further investment might seem ill-advised. But there are risks associated with doing nothing as well as with undergoing change.

Be realistic about the prospects for improvement if nothing changes. Just maintaining the status quo may involve significant resources, in many ways. You may be incurring a staff-time overhead as people work around ill-defined procedures or spend time 'fire-fighting'. Staff may be solving the same problems in different areas of the organisation because there is no coherent strategy for sharing knowledge.

You will also need to be aware of what might be around the corner if you do not change. For example, if your existing IT systems come to the end of their economic life, staying at the baseline will imply replacing them with something that replicates the same functionality, possibly at some cost to your organisation. If the volume of work you have to handle increases, your capacity may not be enough. In situations like these, a 'do nothing' strategy may end up forcing the organisation into a position of unplanned change when a crisis point is reached.

You must consider carefully the real costs and implications of 'doing nothing' if you propose it as an option. However, it may be that after careful consideration it does emerge as the best option; for example, change may be simply too risky or costly for your organisation at the present time.

The other reason for analysing the baseline carefully is to provide the basis for measuring the costs and benefits of other options. It gives a clear picture of the present levels of cost, benefit and risk, so that they can be compared with those of the other options. When you come to specify the benefits you expect from change, this is the starting point for measuring them. If one of the benefits you are hoping for is (for example) improved staff morale, then it will be helpful to have a way to quantify present morale so that future morale can be quantified – perhaps through the number of complaints made by staff.

4.2 What needs to change?

Having established where the organisation is, you need to scope the change: to ask, at a general level, 'what do we want to change?' Scoping the change does not mean creating detailed plans for change; that will come at a later stage. There may be many areas of uncertainty, particularly for far-reaching changes.

Scoping should give a clearer view of the implications of the proposed change – an understanding of the change's anticipated effects on the organisation and its environment. The change may affect the following aspects of the organisation:

- **strategy**: how the proposed change supports the business and IT strategies of the organisation, and how those strategies may need to be developed further to reflect the possible outcomes of the change

- **structure**: how the proposed change will affect the physical and organisational structure of the organisation, its functions and processes and their relationships, and the products and services it delivers

- **management processes**: the impact of the change on the management and planning controls and processes, sources of power and influence, responsibilities, reporting arrangements, performance management, information flows and control mechanisms

- **individuals and roles**: the effect of the change on those involved, including the roles and responsibilities of individuals and workgroups, the effect on requirements for skills, training and job flexibility, and the cultural impact of the change – changes in values, behaviours and attitudes

- **technology**: the requirements for new or different IT, facilities for communication and information management, policies and procedures for IT, and the sourcing and management of IT facilities.

Defining the boundaries

Before considering what will change, how, and who will be affected, it is important to define the boundaries of the change. Effecting any organisational change can be problematic. Organisations are complex systems of people, structures, technology, culture, processes and management, operating in an environment that is itself complex and constantly changing. A change in any one of these elements can have repercussions elsewhere, and the unintended consequences of even minor changes can, in the worst case, destabilise the whole change effort.

Defining the boundaries of the change will help to restrict the problems encountered to 'difficulties' rather than 'messes', as discussed in the introduction. Rather than embarking on a 'mess' – an unbounded, unfocused change effort where neither the starting point nor the objectives are clear – try to ensure that all problems are foreseeable and that they can be considered as 'difficulties'.

If the change programme is too large or unmanageable, consider breaking it down into more easily achievable modules, or approaching the end result by increments. It would be better to cross a river successfully than sink without trace in an ocean. More details on modular and incremental change process are given in chapter 6.

The organisational context You will also need to examine the organisational and business context, which will affect the organisation's ability to achieve change. Some of these issues will already have been encountered when considering the drivers for change that act upon the organisation. They include:

- the readiness of the organisation to respond to the changes required to resolve the problem or grasp the opportunity in this change programme

- the capacity and capability of the organisation to make the change happen

- the extent to which contextual factors can directly affect or influence the outcome of the change – including constraints and obstacles to change, such as geography (a business split between several sites)

- the relationship between this change and other change initiatives under way or planned

- the understanding, by everyone involved in or affected by the change, of the implications of the desired outcome, and their ability to contribute appropriately.

If the change process has been initiated as a result of the development or review of the organisation's IT strategy, much of this activity will probably have been undertaken as part of that development, as described in the companion guide *How to manage Business and IT Strategies.*

Here you may begin to see some divergence between your change goal and what can realistically be achieved through this particular process of change. Limiting factors – anything from your organisation's culture to time and economic constraints – will begin to limit the scope of the change. The scoping phase is important because it allows you to acknowledge the limits that must be placed on your change process – before you actually commit resources.

4.3 Prioritisation

There may be more than one change initiative planned, with a risk of conflicting priorities and only finite resources. It may be that you need to decide which programmes or projects should go ahead now, and which can wait. The process of assessing the relative importance of two or more proposals is known as prioritisation.

In any organisation there are limited resources available. Prioritisation should enable you to allocate those resources to projects or programmes that provide maximum value to your business. The objective is to obtain a list of possible initiatives in descending order of importance. This list gives an indication of the priority of various business demands. Changes in business need and conflicting resource demands will have a subsequent impact on this list.

Why prioritise?

Prioritising a range of possible change initiatives should be conducted in the light of evolving business needs. The process should be systematic and consistent, and should always put business needs first.

At a general level, prioritisation serves to put investment decisions on a rational rather than an arbitrary footing – reason enough to build it into any examination of candidates for change. Other benefits of prioritisation include:

- in the IT arena, systems investment is aligned with business need rather than technical expedience or the appeal of the new (doing what you should, not what you could)

- the organisation makes best use of scarce resources and invests wisely

- the perceived values and risks associated with different proposals are discussed between business managers and suppliers so that any issues that might arise are managed. The different communities of user, manager and IT provider may have very different views on the benefits, costs and risks of a course of action

- justification, documentation and audit are made easier by using a systematic process. Your thinking about prioritisation could feed into the process of constructing a business case (see section 7.5)

- the risk of missing business opportunities can be reduced. Changes that have less worth or positive impact on the business can be deferred in favour of others that will have the greatest possible impact – perhaps 'quick win' changes (see section 6.5) that will make a visible difference to your business and generate enthusiasm for further changes

- when a number of changes are on the table, prioritisation lets you map out a clear direction for your organisation and avoid inappropriate deviations from the strategic direction.

How to prioritise

There are several ways to consider or quantify the importance of different proposals. Some are highly mathematical, involving numerical weightings for the different attributes of propositions. Others, like the 'pain/gain matrix' described overleaf, are more subjective. Although you should never be less than logical and rational about your prioritisation, how you do it is less important than the fact you do it at all. Simply making a list of the proposed changes in the order you plan to make them will help to focus thoughts on the consequences of doing certain things before others.

A related topic is benefits management (see section 8.1). Some benefits of change prepare the ground for other, dependent benefits. Some changes build on the results of earlier change efforts. Prioritisation is an integral part of deciding which benefits need to be achieved first.

Figure 4
Pain/gain matrix

The pain/gain matrix, used to help decide which initiatives should be implemented first

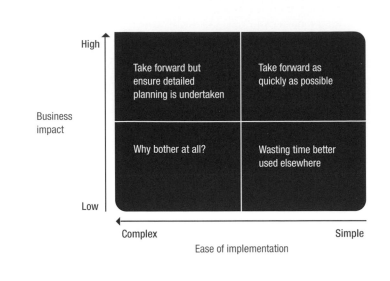

One approach to prioritisation is the 'pain/gain' matrix, shown in Figure 4. This can be used to decide which initiatives should be implemented earliest. Each candidate for action can be assessed against two factors:

- the extent of the benefits to the business that the development will realise

- the difficulty or complexity of achieving the desired outcome and the amount of effort required.

Options near the bottom left of the matrix are complex or difficult to achieve and fail to deliver much benefit, prompting questions about whether they are worth pursuing at all. At the opposite corner, options that deliver significant benefit and are easy to take forward should be moved forward as quickly as possible. They could be 'quick win' changes as discussed in section 6.5 – changes that rapidly deliver clear-cut benefits that can be used to generate enthusiasm and commitment for further changes.

Changes in the bottom right of the matrix are simple to effect but have low impact. It may be that resources are better directed to other change efforts, at least in the short term. Changes in the top left of the matrix are probably worthwhile, but their complexity means detailed planning is required in advance.

Other initiatives

Other initiatives currently in progress could affect the progress of the change or changes you decide to go ahead with. Part of the prioritisation process should be to ensure that these other initiatives have been fully taken into account. There could be implications for your change if finite resources in vital components of your organisation are already committed elsewhere (or soon will be). IT departments, for example, might already be in the process of implementing changes for another department, or troubleshooting in the aftermath of a change. Your contingency plans could include scaling down or delaying part of the planned programme of change.

4.4 Examples of large change programmes

The Inland Revenue's change programme, first introduced in 1993, is making fundamental changes to the way the department is organised, its operations and its management. It incorporates over 20 major projects within its overall scope, one of which is the introduction of self-assessment.

The high-level mission statement of this programme is summed up in four key areas, known as the 'four Cs':

- **customer service** – to gain a significant improvement in customer service by getting people's tax affairs right first time

- **compliance** – to gain a steady improvement in compliance; with the right amount of tax paid at the right time by the right people

- **cost efficiency** – to gain a significant reduction in costs and provide value for money in everything the department does

- **caring for staff** – to recognise that people are the department's most important asset.

The detailed plan of action based on these goals has four themes:

- reorganising the office structure

- simplifying and streamlining work processes

- making better use of information technology

- changing the department's culture in the way people and work are managed.

These statements contain both general goals for the Inland Revenue as a whole and high-level scoping of the change.

Private sector examples   Some examples of major change in the private sector include:

- introduction of online banking services in high street clearing banks

- merger of insurance companies Commercial & General and Norwich Union, requiring common processes for handling insurance business, supported by an integrated IT infrastructure

- changing from a number of service providers to one strategic partner providing support services worldwide for Rolls-Royce and its subsidiaries.

This section deals with assessing the organisation's readiness for change. You are seeking to answer the question 'are we ready for change?'

Within that question are issues around the nature of organisations, their cultures, and the IT that supports them. Key concepts here are stakeholders in change and the risks associated with change.

5.1 Is your organisation ready?

Are some organisations easier to change than others? There are many factors that have a bearing on the answer to this question. Size, structure, technology used, and the relationship with the business environment all play a part. The culture of the organisation will also have a major influence, including staff attitudes and behaviours, personalities and relationships, power structures, and even national characteristics.

Unitary and pluralist organisations

A useful distinction in assessing how prepared your organisation is for change is that between 'unitary' and 'pluralist' organisations.

In a 'unitary' organisation, all members hold a common view of objectives, and are committed to working together in support of those objectives. Authority is vested in those appointed to positions of power, and conflict is seen as dysfunctional. Decisions are taken on a purely rational basis.

In a 'pluralist' organisation, 'politics' and personalities have much more influence. There may be many sources of power other than the recognised authority figures – for example, the 'expert power' exercised by those with particular skills or knowledge. Conflict is seen as inevitable and something to be managed, possibly leading to beneficial outcomes. Decisions are taken as a result of processes of negotiation, compromise and accommodation.

Table 2 outlines the ways in which the two kinds of organisation deal with the issues of interests, conflict and power.

It is difficult to imagine an organisation that is not 'pluralist' to some extent. A 'unitary' organisation might be envisaged when devising the change goal discussed in chapter 3 – an ideal to aim for, but unlikely to be realised.

When planning your change, you will need to guard against making too many 'unitary' assumptions about the culture of your organisation, and ensure that you have taken account of all the 'pluralist' realities with which you will have to contend – conflicts of interest, multiple power sources, and so on.

A 'unitary' approach to change will assume that change can be imposed by legitimate authority, and will be accepted by the organisation as a necessary objective. Management will assume that all members of the organisation will be committed to the change by virtue of their support for the power structure and their willingness to maintain unity. Taking this kind of approach in an organisation that is really a 'pluralist' one is unlikely to be effective.

The processes of decision-making will also influence the approach to change. Experience suggests that change efforts are more successful in those organisations in which there is a high degree of participation by members of staff in decision-making – one of the hallmarks of the 'pluralist' organisation.

Table 2:
Contrast between 'unitary' and 'pluralist' organisations

Contrast between 'unitary' and 'pluralist' organisations in the way they deal with issues of interests, conflict and power

	The 'unitary' view	The 'pluralist' view
Interests	All members share common objectives. There is consensus on the goals of the organisation and the means of achieving them. All members are united in working for organisational success.	There is a multiplicity of interests amongst individuals and groups. Some of these interests will coincide with the formal objectives of the organisation, but some will not.
Conflict	Conflict is unlikely. When it occurs it is dysfunctional and probably malicious. It can be suppressed by management action by the appropriate authority.	Conflict is inevitable and must be expected. Individuals, informal groups and organisational units will differ and will pursue their own interests. Conflict can be managed and directed to beneficial ends.
Power	Legitimate power is exercised by those appointed to authority in the organisational structure. Power resides in those designated to specific positions.	There are many sources of power in the organisation. They all have a part to play in the development of the organisation and in the resolution of conflict.

Organisational complexity　　A central issue is organisational complexity. Any attempt to implement a change in one area may have consequences elsewhere. Acknowledging and taking account of organisational complexity is one of the critical success factors for successful change.

For example, a change programme aimed at introducing IT facilities to improve internal administrative efficiency and productivity may conflict with an existing programme of staff redeployment (human resource development) or may cut across well-established arrangements for assignment of tasks in the organisation (preservation and stability). Similarly, the introduction of new customer-oriented services may create problems for the staffing function (human resource development), but generate opportunities for reduced overheads (productivity and efficiency).

Recognising organisational complexity is one of the critical success factors for any change effort. The complexity of organisational change should never be underestimated, and as you now move into identifying what might be attempted as part of the change effort, this consideration becomes paramount.

The management of change can be seen as a complex undertaking, because of the systemic or 'holistic' nature of organisational change. As soon as the organisation moves beyond very simple changes, it needs to take account of a variety of interrelated factors.

The principles for understanding organisational change can be summarised as follows:

- **organisms, not machines**: organisations are organisms: they are not like machines, with parts that can be changed and reassembled at will. Members of the organisation will have views on the desirability of the proposed changes, and must be consulted

- **occupational and political systems**: recognise that organisations are occupational and political systems as well as systems for the rational allocation of resources. Rational arguments alone will not be enough to carry forward change. The implications for the occupational and political systems must also be considered

- **simultaneous operation**: all members of an organisation operate simultaneously in all three systems – the rational, occupational and political. All three types of arguments must be given weight. An individual's position will combine considerations of all three types.

Another aspect of organisational complexity that must be considered is the relationship of the change programme to other programmes and initiatives taking place in the organisation. Organisations are often involved in several projects or programmes, at local or corporate level, which could be competing for resources, management time and the involvement of staff. The various programmes and initiatives could even be pulling in different directions and conflicting with each other. Careful consideration must be given to the interaction of programmes in the organisation, and the ways in which they can be reconciled and integrated.

Dealing with uncertainty

In an ideal world, the change programme would be based on a clear statement of the desired outcomes, a clear understanding of the actions required to achieve them and a stable environment in which to work towards them. However, in many situations, and particularly those involving anything other than the simplest of changes, you will have to work in a less certain world.

In any situation involving organisational change, there will be different perspectives on the change and its objectives. The various stakeholders could well have differing views on the importance of the various aspects of the change programme. For example, the views of management and staff could differ on the objectives for the introduction of new IT-based facilities; or there could be differences of opinion among business functions on the requirements for a structural reorganisation. Or business partners (or others 'joined up' with the organisation) may not be prepared or able to change in line with your requirements.

There may be conflicts between the various forces (drivers) acting within the organisation, as already discussed. External stakeholders such as customers and key suppliers may also have influential views. Thus, although there may appear to be a clear focus for the change effort, there may still be disagreement over the details.

For any given objective, whether or not there is a consensus view in favour of it, the question arises, 'what needs to be done as part of the change effort to ensure that this objective is achieved?' The question is one of cause and effect: 'to what extent can we be sure that if we proceed with a certain course of action, the desired consequences will follow?'

This question is particularly difficult to answer if the focus of the desired change is on policy outcomes. This topic is discussed in more detail in the companion volume *How to manage Performance*.

If the proposed course of action is to be effective, the organisation will need to be sure that:

- the inputs to the change process will produce the desired outputs

- the outputs will lead to the production of the desired final outcomes.

Figure 5 shows the two dimensions of uncertainty with which the organisation may have to deal:

- lack of agreement on the objectives of the change effort

- lack of certainty about cause and effect in the change activities.

Figure 5 Dimensions of uncertainty	With high agreement on objectives and certainty about cause and effect, success should be relatively easy. Low values of either or both aspects will add difficulty and complexity to the change effort

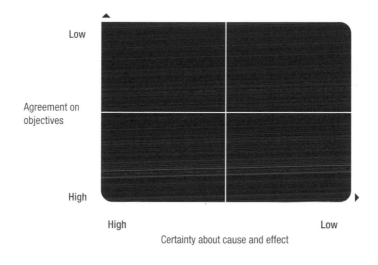

The situation in the bottom left-hand quadrant – high agreement on objectives, and high certainty about cause and effect – suggests that the change effort will be well defined and relatively easy to plan. This may well apply, for example, to 'corrective' changes. For more complex changes, the situation is more likely to be that in the upper right-hand quadrant. Here, the change effort will have to confront varying expectations and deal with the uncertainties involved in the achievement of objectives. In this situation, consider how the change will be achieved, including the possibility of incremental change and pilot or demonstration studies, both of which are dealt with in chapters 6 and 7.

At this stage of making high-level plans, be sure that you fully take account of the level of uncertainty you are dealing with. Having been through a process of stock-taking, you should have no illusions about the present state of your organisation. This should form a sound basis for assessing how certain you can be that the plans you make now will achieve what you are hoping for.

Techniques for moving from the low/low quadrant to the high/high quadrant include managing risks, reducing risk by taking more cautious approaches to change such as modular and incremental methods, and setting up pilot programmes before a gradual change. These methods are discussed in chapters 6 and 7.

Inter-organisational complexity in the public sector

The boundaries between organisations in the public sector, and between the public and private sectors, are blurring. For some time the private sector has been taking over functions previously carried out within the public sector, particularly in IT service delivery. Public-Private Partnerships are an option for achieving value for money in the public sector, and in the delivery of public services. Many policy and service changes are delivered through a multitude of local authority, voluntary, academic and private sector organisations.

Increasingly, there is a movement towards the co-operation of multiple public sector organisations in the delivery of services to the public. One of the objectives of *Modernising Government* is to ensure that government is responsive to the citizen and is, from the public's point of view, seamless. This involves working across organisational boundaries, and the government is actively encouraging initiatives to establish partnership delivery by all parts of the public sector, involving the private sector where appropriate.

Examples of public/private sector collaboration include:

- Ordnance Survey, working with a large number of partners to provide maps that meet individual business needs, such as local authorities, national industries, corporate and commercial customers

- the Planning Inspectorate's Planning Portal, which will be a general planning advisory service linking the public, business and other users of the planning system to a wide range of advice, guidance and services on planning and related topics. The service will be accessed via a single managed internet portal that will link all relevant organisations

- the Department for Education and Skills' Connexions initiative, which will create a single point of access for 13–19 year olds to help them prepare for the transition to work and adult life. Connexions will help to integrate careers, health and youth services, as well as other support services, so young people no longer have to deal with up to eight different agencies to get the support they need.

Where multiple organisations come together in networks to deliver services to each other or to the public, changes in one organisation may well have implications for other organisations in the network. Where business processes are closely integrated across organisations, it is harder to restrict the focus of the change process to a single organisation. Management of change in a network of organisations is more complex than in a single organisation. Issues that can arise in this situation may involve:

- differences in perception – about the kind of changes required, the roles of the various organisations, the new services to be offered, the target recipients, the objectives of the new service, or the business processes to be implemented

- problems related to the mandates of the respective organisations: what they are allowed to change, what they are obliged or choose to do, and the statutory requirements for their operations or the delivery of services

- differences in culture between the organisations – risk-averse/entrepreneurial

- differences in the willingness or ability of the organisations to absorb change, their skills and capabilities, and the pace at which change can be introduced

- differences in planning horizons, human resource policies, budgeting and accounting procedures, and procedures for performance management and business case development.

These factors will need to be taken into consideration when planning a management of change exercise involving several organisations.

5.2 Is the culture ready?

In any change effort, of any size, the importance of 'taking people with you' must not be underestimated. People will have views on the proposed change, and may not feel that their interests are best served by it. They may even see reason to resist or obstruct the change. You should take time to consider the implications of the proposed change for the culture of your organisation. For many changes, the culture outside the organisation may be equally important; for example, the attitudes of your clients or customers may need to be changed if you are planning to provide a radically new service for them.

Culture can be summed up as 'the way we do things around here'. Organisations define and order themselves 'top-down' by means of hierarchies, job descriptions, lines of command, business strategies and other formal devices. But as anyone who has worked in an organisation of almost any size knows, this is only half the story. The other side of the coin is the unwritten rules, power struggles, personality clashes, rivalries, pecking orders, rumours, and history that make up the organisation's culture. An entrenched culture can persist for many years, through thick and thin, in spite of personnel changes, even against the will of senior management.

Clearly the culture of an organisation can be a formidable obstacle to change, and should not be underestimated in the planning of a change effort. Be aware also that a highly radical change may simply be too far-reaching for the culture to absorb, even though the drivers for change and your vision for the future make it clear that it is necessary. If so, consider whether a series of modular or incremental changes might be more appropriate (see chapter 6).

Taking account of past change initiatives

Take account of recent change efforts and their results, particularly those that failed, succeeded incompletely, or had detrimental effects on morale. They are in the past and beyond your control, and should not have an influence on the strategic basis for a change programme, but they are vital in considering what the culture of the organisation can stand in terms of change.

If staff feel that recent changes were not successful, they may be resistant to further changes. Similar feelings may be engendered by change that was perceived as being handed down from 'on high' rather than based on grass-roots requirements. In such cases, the requirements for communication, training staff and overcoming resistance (set out in chapter 7) will be even more important to the success of the change process.

It may also be simply too soon for a far-reaching change; if a radical change has recently been implemented, whatever its perceived or actual success, it may be too soon to attempt further change on such a scale. Again, consider a modular approach to 'soften the blow'.

Changing attitudes and behaviour

Identify the people who will be affected by the change, and the changes you would like to make to their way of working. You may wish to change:

- their knowledge

- their attitudes

- individual behaviour

- organisational or group behaviour.

Imparting knowledge is relatively easy. There are many ways of informing people about the change, what is expected of them, and changes in procedures or work processes. However, the transfer of knowledge does not guarantee that it has been adequately understood or accepted, or that it will be acted upon.

There is some debate about the relationship between attitudes and behaviour, and about whether the above list represents the order in which aspects of organisational culture can be changed. Should the organisation try to change attitudes before it can expect changes in behaviour? One approach suggests that as a first step it is necessary to ensure that people's attitudes have been changed, and that they have accepted and 'internalised' the need for change. They will then be receptive to the need to change their behaviour in line with the change programme. According to this view, a change in attitude must precede a permanent change in behaviour.

An alternative view is that when people are put into an environment where their behaviour is required to change, and the change in behaviour is enforced, their attitudes will follow and they will gradually accept and internalise the change. While it is accepted that attitudes influence behaviour, it can be true that behaviour influences attitudes.

A similar argument applies to changes in organisational or group behaviour. Attempting to change the attitudes of all relevant staff as a precursor to making the change may be difficult and unnecessary. It may be more effective to introduce the changes in tasks, roles and responsibilities and ensure that they are properly carried out (through training and preparation); changes in attitudes should then follow.

5.3 Stakeholders

In this context, a stakeholder is any body or person, within or beyond your organisation, who will be affected by the proposed change.

For a public sector body, the stakeholders are likely to be:

- bodies that can assign resources, such as HM Treasury, the sponsoring department for an agency, bodies awarding grants, customers who can assign resources in return for services

- bodies that can exercise political influence, such as Members of Parliament, pressure groups, the media, the general public, the Trade Union Side

- bodies involved in business relationships, such as customers, service providers, contractors and strategic partners

- bodies which can exert other influences, such as local authorities, industry groups, regulatory bodies

- businesses and citizens

- internal stakeholders: the management and staff of the organisation.

For the NHS, relevant stakeholders would include Primary Care Trusts and Community Health Councils; for local authorities, stakeholders would typically include local community groups, social services and the police.

For a private sector company, the stakeholders are likely to be:

- bodies involved in business relationships, such as customers, service providers, outsourcing partners, contractors

- internal stakeholders at a general level: for example, shareholders, the board of directors, the chief executive, steering committees and so on

- internal staff: committees or departments that control the assignment of resources, including human resources

- internal stakeholders: the management and staff of the company

It may be that some of the stakeholder groups from the public sector list are also relevant to private sector organisations.

A vital component of the change process is identifying stakeholders and taking account of their views on the change. The aim is to bring everyone who has a stake in the change on board and make them feel not only that they are part of the change but that they will benefit from it as well.

In any change situation there will be those who support the change and those who oppose it. There will be those who gain from it and those who lose – and those who are convinced they will lose despite all evidence to the contrary. There will be those who anticipate an opportunity and those who see only a threat. And of course there will be those who are indifferent to the change; this may turn out to be helpful or unhelpful, depending on the influence they have. Stakeholders' positions are also likely to be linked to the amount of change they themselves will have to make.

Stakeholders' positions may be rational and justifiable, or emotional and unfounded, but they must all be taken into account since by definition they can all affect the change process. In some cases stakeholders have the power to insist that the change takes place or to determine or influence the desired outcome. Not all stakeholders are equally important; they should be considered in terms of the amount of influence they can bring to bear, and their sympathy with the aims and objectives of the change exercise.

It may be possible to mobilise influential stakeholders who are supportive of the change, to help in overcoming the resistance of those who oppose it. They would become 'change champions'; individuals who are nominated as 'prime movers' of the change (see section 7.6).

Internal stakeholders are critically important for the success of the exercise. You will need to identify internal stakeholders and pinpoint differences of opinion within the organisation on the change. Staff who are opposed to the change can be co-opted on to analysis or design teams, or invited to join task forces or focus groups. This should help to convince staff of the necessity for change; they will become part of the solution and therefore more likely to support the change.

The public as stakeholder in public sector change

An important group of stakeholders to consider for public sector organisations is the general public. They can make their views known in a variety of ways – directly, and through political groups, special interest groups, consumer organisations, patient representative organisations, and so on. Service delivery organisations need to ensure that those who use their services will be satisfied with the outcome of changes that will affect them. The views of the public can be obtained through activities such as surveys and citizens' panels.

Those who deal with the public will also have a view. The change management programme must be prepared to deal with a complex situation involving professional affiliations, career aspirations, views on client service, and the status of professionals as 'independent experts'. It may take considerable time and effort to achieve a consensus over the scope of the necessary changes and their implementation.

OGC's guidance on programme management provides practical advice on stakeholder management, including:

- identifying key stakeholders from the groups of people managing and working within the change initiative, together with people or organisations directly or indirectly contributing to or affected by the change

- analysing the stakeholders and their specific areas of interest in order to manage their expectations effectively

- effective communications with stakeholders to ensure their continuing co-operation and support through a good understanding of the change initiative and its progress.

For more detail, consult the complementary guide *Managing Successful Programmes*.

5.4 Risk

Risks are uncertain outcomes. Risks are not necessarily negative; they may represent positive opportunities as well as negative threats. Risk management is a recognised management discipline that has many applications throughout business. In the context of change, risk management is concerned with analysing those results of change that are uncertain, and with minimising their probability or impact if they are negative.

Risk management involves having processes in place to identify and then monitor risks; access to reliable, up-to-date information about risks; the right balance of control in place to deal with those risks; and decision-making processes supported by a framework of risk analysis and evaluation.

Levels of risk

There are four levels of risk:

- strategic: risks involved in ensuring business survival and long-term security or stability of the organisation

- programme: risks involved in managing interdependencies between individual projects and the wider business environment

- projects: risks involved in making progress against project plans

- operational: risks involved in technical problems, supplier management and so on.

Higher levels of risk feed into those levels below them; strategic risks will have implications at all the other levels, while operational risks are localised and limited in scope. A risk may materialise initially at one level but subsequently have a major impact at a different level. A recent example is a high street bank facing technical faults at the operational level; ultimately, customers' confidence in the bank's online service became a strategic risk. This highlights the importance of sharing information throughout the organisation, and of understanding the level of risk that is being faced. If a risk grows outside agreed limits, it should be decided that it no longer represents, say, an operational risk and now may affect the project as a whole.

Depending on the scale of the change you are planning, you will have to analyse risks at one or more of these levels.

Types of risk

Different organisations will face different types of risk. Some types of risk are as follows:

- strategic/commercial risks

- economic/financial/market risks

- legal and regulatory risks

- organisational management/people issues

- political/societal factors

- environmental factors/acts of God (*force majeure*)

- technical/operational/infrastructure risks.

The risk of inaction

As well as gauging the level of risk inherent in your proposed changes, you should also offset the risk of inaction. If you decide that change is too risky and terminate the change process, what will be the result? If things continue as they are, what will eventually happen? Be aware that not changing, or procrastinating, is an action with consequences for your organisation, just as change is. By the time change has become cheaper, easier to achieve or simply inevitable, the change required may be much greater in scope, or so urgent that a step-by-step approach (see chapter 6) is no longer possible.

Responses to risk

When risks have been identified, you will need to evaluate them (assess the probability that they will occur and their potential impact) before deciding what to do about them. How much risk you take will depend on the benefits you hope to achieve, as well as your organisation's cultural attitude to risk and its ability to limit the exposure to risk.

Responses to risk can be to:

- manage down the risk by taking actions to prevent the risk occurring

- transfer some aspects of the risk – perhaps by paying a third party to take it on (a major feature of the Private Finance Initiative); note that business and reputational risk cannot be transferred

- tolerate the risk – perhaps because nothing can be done at a reasonable cost to mitigate it

- treat the risk – take action to control it in some way

- terminate the risk – by doing things differently and thus removing the risk, where it is feasible to do so.

Further details on risk management are given in the OGC Risk Guidelines and in the complementary guides *Managing Successful Programmes* and *Managing Successful Projects with PRINCE 2*.

5.5 Is the IT infrastructure ready?

In today's business environment, whether in the public or private sector, it has practically become a given that IT will be involved in change. Information systems, information technology, telecommunications and the internet have moved from being administrative tools, through supporting management processes, to the stage where they can be enablers and even drivers for profound change. The implications of this for those planning change are significant.

IT and business transformation

In previous eras an IT-related change would have meant automating an existing process, or managing existing information in a more efficient way – corrective or content-driven changes. Today, new technologies can exert an overriding pressure for change, or suggest dramatic changes to the services a business can offer and the manner in which it provides them. Internet banking and shopping and online links to income tax assessments are all recent examples of this.

If you are planning to take advantage of any of these developments in your organisation, whether it is to do something better or to do something new, you must ensure that you are fully prepared for the changes implied for your organisation's IT. This means being aware of the implications for your IT infrastructure, now and in the future. A failure to deal with these issues can actually lead to future changes being inhibited rather than enabled; the financial consequences can be devastating.

Levels of IT-related change

One method for analysing the different impacts IT can have on the organisation is through the classification developed in MIT's 'Management in the 90s' project, shown in Figure 6. This shows how the role of IT can range from 'localised exploitation' at the lowest level, corresponding to simple automation of discrete business activities – the first stage that was reached historically – to 'business scope redefinition' – transformation of the business, the stage we are at today.

The dividing line between evolution and revolution is also shown. This distinction has already been discussed in chapter 3. At this more detailed planning stage, you need to decide how IT fits in with, or is going to enable, revolutionary change.

Clearly, if you are looking at a change process that will take you above the line into revolution, you will have to give very serious thought to the relationship between your IT strategy and your business strategy.

For more detail on managing IT and business strategies, consult the companion guide *How to manage Business and IT Strategies*.

Scope of IT-related change

Having gauged the level of IT-related change you are contemplating, you must also assess the scope: the areas and operations that will be affected. This will give you a better idea of the starting points for the detailed plans to be made in the next section.

IT-supported change can affect the organisation at one or more levels:

- individual
- workgroup
- business function
- organisational
- inter-organisational.

Figure 6	Degrees of IT-enabled change, from automation of basic tasks (localised exploitation) up to
Degrees of	business scope redefinition. The horizontal line divides evolutionary change from revolutionary
IT-enabled change	change (source: MIT)

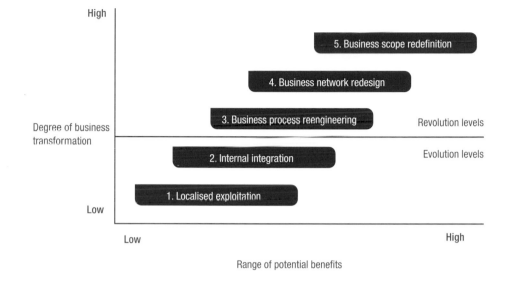

Examples of individual and workgroup changes would be the introduction of facilities such as word processing, automated form-filling, information sharing systems, and communications such as email, all of which serve to improve the efficiency and effectiveness of staff at a local level. Changing business function involves redesigning business processes with the help of IT. Organisational and inter-organisational change means high-level changes to functions, processes, methods of service delivery and communication, through improved communication and information sharing.

Inter-organisational change may also involve realising additional benefits through the integration of information from a variety of sources and the removal of organisational and geographic boundaries.

IT infrastructure   The ability of your organisation to make far-reaching changes could depend on the ability of its IT infrastructure to support and promote them. The infrastructure must be able to accommodate the changes in information systems that will be necessary for your change process. The importance of the IT infrastructure increases as the scope of change widens, from personal up to organisational and inter-organisational.

IT infrastructure includes the following:

- hardware, software and computer-related communications such as internet access and telecommunications links, access and information capture devices

- the people involved in planning, management, implementation and operation

- management and technical policies (which may also include standards, documentation and procedures) that apply to the IT infrastructure

- the supporting environmental infrastructure of specialised buildings, cabling, cable ducts, air conditioning and so on.

Whatever the situation in your organisation, be sure you do not make optimistic assumptions about the scale of infrastructure change required, or the time that will be required to effect it.

If your organisation is to achieve organisation-wide business change, it must be in a position to change the relevant elements of the IT infrastructure. Effecting this change will be easier if the infrastructure is common across the organisation.

If the IT infrastructure is to be redefined, consider the benefits to be gained from defining organisation-wide standards, applications, data architectures, business data models, standards and procedures, and business-critical information systems that are used across more than one department. How much centralisation and standardisation is appropriate depends on the organisation, and of course the work involved in imposing standards on a larger organisation will be correspondingly greater, particularly if a multitude of local standards already exists within it.

Failure to give adequate consideration to the implications of the IT infrastructure can lead to IT becoming an inhibitor rather than an enabler of change. For example, business developments could be held up by the need to replace legacy (outdated) platforms, or to overcome the problems posed by incompatible email systems. The creation of an adaptable organisation-wide infrastructure will minimise this kind of issue. Furthermore, to some extent the IT infrastructure has to be 'future-proof' – prepared for unforeseen, future developments, to the extent that this is possible. Creating, or planning to create, more than you need at the present time may come to be invaluable in years to come.

The 'intelligent customer' role

As well as the physical IT infrastructure, you must take account of those who provide it for you. Your IT service providers will almost certainly be major stakeholders in the change process. You will need to have access to expert advice on the implications for the business if your IT is going to change. In government, the role of the technical adviser to the business is often referred to as the 'intelligent customer', providing the interface between the customer and the provider. The key function of the 'intelligent customer' is an in-depth knowledge of the business combined with realistic understanding of what the provider can – and cannot – do.

The 'intelligent customer' role includes:

- understanding of infrastructure issues

- proactive approaches – working closely with the business to identify new IT opportunities

- readiness to look outside the organisation, reflecting today's emphasis on inter-organisational communication, information interchange and business process integration

- ensuring governance arrangements are adequate for acquiring, implementing and managing IT-based services and their delivery.

The role of central
IT co-ordination

The degree of centralisation of IT infrastructure is for your organisation to decide, taking into account its business functions and their relationship, the structure and management culture of the organisation, and the degree of autonomy that is to be allowed at local levels. Integration of different information systems will always be desirable, but will need to be offset against the facilities that locally specific systems may offer. If the potential benefits of communication and sharing are to be achieved, central co-ordination is advisable for at least the following:

- defining standards and interfaces for IT systems

- defining applications and data architectures for organisation-wide information systems

- implementation of business-critical information systems that are used across multiple business functions

- standards and procedures for IT security and business community

- standards for use of IT platforms, development tools and communications facilities such as email

If your organisation has a range of different infrastructure elements in different areas, making changes to the infrastructure to support business and organisational change will be potentially difficult and expensive. The choice and acquisition of IT infrastructure should take into account the probable need for continuous enhancement and updating to accommodate the requirements for support of business change. Where the choice of IT infrastructure is in the hands of an external service provider, the organisation should ensure that the selected infrastructure will meet the business requirements for future support of change.

The development of infrastructure standards in the public sector, as part of the *Modernising Government* programme, will facilitate intercommunication and data sharing.

Planning an e-business change

You may be planning to take advantage of e-business to revolutionise your business, both in terms of internal efficiency and in terms of improved or radically new services that you could offer. However, the pace of technological change is such that you are, in a sense, aiming for a moving target. By the time the change process is complete, the technologies you have chosen may be dated or even obsolete, particularly if the organisation is large and the change process likely to be lengthy.

Before you embark on a programme of e-business change, you should look carefully at the issues and what others are doing, to determine the particular drivers for change that affect your organisation in this area. Concentrate on three issues:

- what is happening in your business environment in terms of e-business

- how rapidly this is happening

- which e-business models could be adapted for your organisation.

Ideally, your analysis would include a 'snapshot' of e-business factors – drivers for change – in your area and also an indication of the rate of change of each factor. The rate of change may offer most insight into what your response might be. Clearly, organisational and cultural readiness will play a huge part in determining whether your e-business change is feasible. Can you change quickly enough to respond to the challenges of e-business? The risks may be too great to justify the change, or it could be that the potential benefits outweigh them. Or you may feel that your customers will not stay faithful to an organisation that does not embrace e-business. Whatever your situation, do not ignore the pace of change in e-business.

For more information on this topic, see the companion volume *How to manage Business and IT Strategies*.

This section deals with the question 'how can we approach change?'
Often, this will involve a shift of focus from the purely internal to a wider
perspective that includes outsiders – related organisations, suppliers, partners,
customers – as well as a move to considering how the organisation might be seen
'from the outside in'. (An exception to this would be the earlier involvement of
management consultants when taking stock of your current situation.)

You will need to address the issue of how quickly the change has to be brought
about. In the same way as we can distinguish between radical and evolutionary
changes, so we can make a distinction between radical, evolutionary and modular
methods of changing.

6.1 Transformational change

In transformational change (also known as 'big bang' or discontinuous change)
the entire change is planned and implemented in one exercise designed to effect
all the related changes.

Transformational change carries a high degree of risk. A change programme of
high complexity will demand a great deal of effort and management commitment.
You must ensure that your organisation has sufficient capacity and capability for
change before embarking on the change effort, otherwise there is a high risk of
failure. It is estimated that around 70–80% of Business Process Reengineering
(BPR) and Total Quality Management (TQM) exercises, for example, either fail
to meet their objectives or deliver disappointing results.

There will be times when the 'big bang' approach is the only feasible solution.
An example is when the change has to coincide with other developments or
legislative requirements, and a return to the old arrangements is not possible.
There may also be advantages in attempting transformational change when the
desired outcome is clearly defined and agreed, and the tasks to be performed and
the relationships between the various elements of the change are well understood.

Other circumstances that may require transformational change are:

- when many changes must be made simultaneously, as in a major process
  re-engineering implementation, or a corporate reorganisation

- when discontinuous change is used as a means of overcoming resistance,
  which could slow down or inhibit incremental change

- when the organisation wishes to avoid the uncertainties associated with a long
  period of incremental change.

It may be possible to arrange some form of 'parallel running' in which the old and new arrangements co-exist side by side, and the new arrangements are exhaustively tested before implementation.

6.2 Incremental change

An incremental change is achieved gradually, through an evolutionary process. An incremental approach to change, where it is possible, will carry less risk and is more likely to succeed than a transformational change. The desired change is effected through a series of 'manageable chunks' of change; after each step the organisation can assess the results and determine whether the overall objective is still appropriate. Each step in the change process must leave the organisation in a state of equilibrium, from which it can move forward to the next step. In a situation where external pressures are continually shifting, objectives are changing or unclear, and the impact of the changes is difficult to predict, the incremental approach enables management to maintain control over the change process.

This approach does not preclude the possibility of radical change. A radical outcome can be approached incrementally, without incurring the risks of a transformational change process.

Where an incremental approach to transition is possible, the introduction of the new arrangements may be via a phased build-up of functions or facilities, or a gradual roll-out across different units of the organisation, or a combination of these strategies. An incremental approach gives the organisation the opportunity to learn from the early stages of transition and to modify the later stages if necessary.

6.3 Modular change

In modular change the change is broken down into distinct, more easily achievable modules, each of which offers some benefit, even when the others are not yet complete. A module is a discrete 'package' of change that can be isolated from other change efforts.

Adopting a modular and/or incremental approach is a means of reducing risk. However, there are costs. The initial consideration of the best approach to modular or incremental delivery will take management time. There may be delay in the delivery of the business benefits, which needs to be offset by the potential to deliver a subset of business benefits early within the project. Adequately testing the delivered components, individually and in combination, will help to create the expected final entity.

6.4	Interim arrangements

The transition period should be recognised as a distinct state of the organisation, different from both the current and planned future states. It may be necessary to implement interim arrangements for the transition period, including for example:

- organisational structures
- management responsibilities
- programme and project structures
- policies and procedures
- staffing arrangements and use of external services
- arrangements for acquisition and disposal of resources.

Some of the development activities described above could be regarded as contributing to the transition stage.

The transition period is likely to be a time of stress and uncertainty, and planning for the transition must take account of the concerns of those inside and outside the organisation who will be affected or who have a legitimate right to be kept informed.

6.5	'Quick wins'

Where the change effort is spread over a long period, the change strategy should aim for the achievement of a succession of 'quick wins', rather than planning for all the benefits to appear at the end of the programme. A 'quick win' is a benefit achieved from the programme that:

- is visible to the whole organisation
- is a concrete achievement that cannot be disputed
- clearly contributes to the change effort.

The advantages of the 'quick win' strategy are:

- those involved in the change effort can be justifiably rewarded and motivated
- there are ongoing benefits that offset the costs of the change effort
- a succession of 'quick wins' maintains momentum on the programme
- feedback on the achievements helps to keep the change on track
- demonstration of benefits helps to maintain the support of corporate management for the change effort
- delivery of benefits helps to overcome resistance to the change effort.

There are similarities with a modular approach; those modules achieved early on in a modular change programme would be similar to 'quick wins'. If you decide on a modular approach, consider which modules might be most advantageous in cultural terms to tackle first, in the sense of generating interest, support or enthusiasm.

6.6 Programme management

There will always be links and interdependencies between change processes and other initiatives taking place in the organisation and perhaps beyond. Where there is complexity of this kind, you should adopt a programme management approach.

Programme management is an approach that recognises that the path to achieving the desired outcome cannot be rigorously specified in advance, and will be subject to deviations and changes of direction. It helps to organise, manage, accommodate and control these changes so that the eventual outcome meets the objectives of organisational change.

A programme will be made up of a number of projects, which between them will deliver the desired outcome. Each could have its change owner, and might perhaps be broken down in its turn into modules or incremental levels.
In addition, the projects may be organised into 'tranches' that are completed step by step, each tranche delivering another set of benefits.

For full guidance on programme management, consult the complementary guide *Managing Successful Programmes*.

Making it happen

This chapter deals with answering the question 'how will we achieve the change?' – the implementation of the change, with an emphasis on the cultural aspects of making a change happen.

7.1 The stages of implementation

The implementation phase can be considered as covering three stages of activity: development, transition and operation.

Development

Development means designing and creating new procedures, structural arrangements, behaviours and systems. Where organisational changes are required, the development activity may require the production of new policies, procedure manuals, process descriptions, service delivery arrangements and so on.

An important aspect of the development period will be the preparation of the staff who will be affected by the change, through training, issue of publicity material, and involvement in the design, planning and development. Adequate communication with staff will be a key determinant of the success of the change effort.

Transition

If you opt for 'big bang' change, the transition period will be brief and probably highly disruptive in terms of business operation – possibly to the extent that no work is possible during the period. An example would be the replacement or installation of a new physical IT network in an organisation already reliant on such a network. The organisation would not be able to function as normal during transition.

If you opt for modular change, the transition period will be longer and punctuated by the advent of the benefits for each module. There will also be 'breathing spaces' after each module during which you can take stock and almost certainly learn some lessons from what has happened. Although there will be disruption, it will be localised, and there will only be interruptions to business operation where vital functions – or those through which all work must pass – are affected. Staff in modules currently unaffected by change will be watching carefully; it is important that those who are affected have positive things to say about the change effort.

The situation will be similar in an incremental change process: a longer transition period, characterised by some local disruption but overall continuity. Lessons can be learned at any stage and aspects of the change transition 'tweaked' to smooth its progress. Again, remember the importance of the culture. Keep the change moving, and ensure that its benefits are visible and well known.

Operation

Following a successful transition, the new arrangements become operational. The change effort must be continued into the operational period, to ensure that the change is maintained once the transition activities are completed. The organisation must be 'refrozen' in its new configuration – the change must be institutionalised.

Organisational change may involve changes in the relationships between parts of the organisation, and between the organisation and external providers. These could involve the introduction of formal Service Level Agreements, the transfer of service responsibility to external providers, the implementation of new services for customers, or the development of services delivered jointly with other organisations. The implications of these changes are discussed in the companion guide *How to manage Service Provision.*

It is unlikely that plans developed for the change effort will survive without modification. The activities of the change programme itself could have unanticipated consequences for the organisation, its technology or its environment (including customers). In addition, there may well be changes occurring inside and outside the organisation that have to be accommodated in the plans. It will be necessary to keep the plans under constant review, and to be prepared to review the details to correct minor deviations or, more radically, to review the objectives and desired outcomes of the change effort.

The activities of monitoring and control are discussed in more detail in the companion guide *How to manage Performance.*

7.2 Before and after the change

Unfreezing and refreezing

For any organisational change, the change programme must extend beyond the implementation period. In order to ensure that the change will be accepted by the people concerned, and will endure, the change programme must include the activities leading up to the change, and – just as important – the activities that follow up the change. This is expressed in the model of change suggested by Lewin, which identifies three stages in the process of organisational change:

- unfreezing

- making the change – implementation

- refreezing.

The 'unfreezing' phase is concerned with preparation for the change. The intention of this phase is to decrease people's commitment to the current procedures and make them aware of the need for the change, to counter resistance, and to generate support in favour of the change.

Existing attitudes and beliefs are 'unfrozen' in preparation for the change, so that people will be receptive to it when it takes place. Activities are likely to include:

- a programme of communication to ensure that all those concerned are kept fully informed

- involvement of staff in planning and preparation

- training and support for staff who will be affected by the change

- publicity campaigns to reinforce key messages about the change

- identifying and addressing resistance to the change.

The change itself will take place in accordance with the programme or project plan, and will build on the preparation activities of the 'unfreezing' phase. The activities in this phase are described in the companion guide *How to manage Service Acquisition.*

The 'refreezing' phase can be critical to the success of the change effort – yet it is often neglected. It cannot be assumed that the changes introduced in the implementation phase will be maintained as planned without positive action by management. The changes need to be institutionalised, and the organisation 'refrozen' in the new configuration. Consideration needs to be given to:

- leading from the front: demonstration by senior management that they have embraced and are supporting the change

- control and monitoring to ensure that the changes have taken place as planned and are being maintained

- follow up on new procedures to ensure that they are being followed correctly

- continuing support to staff as they increase their familiarisation with the changes, such as through helpdesks and training

- reinforcing changed attitudes and behaviours; for example, through publicity and reward mechanisms such as rewards for appropriate behaviour

- the application of sanctions to discourage inappropriate behaviours

- changing the language and terminology used in the organisation – for example, by getting staff to refer to 'customers' instead of 'users'

- the redeployment or removal of staff who are particularly resistant to change or who are being obstructive to the change effort

- the recruitment of staff who are expected to be sympathetic to the new configuration and are able to contribute positively to it

- continuing positive efforts to eliminate pre-change behaviours.

This process of change can be related to the Force Field analysis technique described earlier. In the 'unfreezing' phase, the existing structure of forces is disturbed, and in the 'refreezing' phase a new configuration of forces, supportive of the new situation, is maintained in place. Part of the 'refreezing' task is to ensure that the old restraining forces do not regain their former influence.

The following processes may be of use to 'refreeze' the organisation around the change:

- **socialisation**: ensuring that the change is assimilated into the beliefs, preferences, norms and values of the members of the target organisation. The need to socialise new members of the organisation is highly important. Belief systems must be continually supported

- **commitment**: persuading members to assume 'ownership' of the change and to internalise it as a part of their own system of preferences. Ensure that commitment exists through all levels of the organisation

- **rewards**: action to reward successes in performing the new behaviours associated with the change. Recognition should be immediate and public. A mix of rewards may be required over time. Rewards must be perceived as equitable by staff. Strive for minimum conflict

- **diffusion**: dual strategies of maintenance and growth by transferring changes established in one unit to a new unit or units. Spreading institutionalised behaviours into several sub-systems tends to affirm change behaviour and protect against setbacks

- **sustained sponsorship**: stress the need to maintain sponsorship during changes in leadership or top management. Weakened sponsorship will create a climate to return to a previous steady state. Messages from sponsors should consistently reinforce the values and beliefs of the intervention

- **reinforcement**: variations in institutionalised behaviour over time must be identified and reinforced if they are consistent with the desired change. If counterforces are detected, one or more of the above processes must be used to check possible decline.

Second-order effects

You should also be alert to the possibility of change, once implemented, having second-order effects that may lead to suggestions for further changes in the business or organisation. It is commonplace for changes to lead to further unanticipated changes once the implications of the original change have worked themselves through. Possible unanticipated effects of change might be:

- desired changes not being achieved

- changes working out differently from expected

- changes taking place which were not anticipated

- the changed situation giving rise to additional unforeseen changes.

Even where the desired changes are achieved successfully, there may be 'second-order' effects that can prevent the organisation from 'refreezing' in the desired new configuration. For example, the introduction of a new IT system may appear to deliver the desired benefits of increased efficiency, but there may be second-order consequences on a human level, affecting issues such as job security, career opportunities, stress, and individuals' status and autonomy within the organisation.

This kind of 'knock-on effect' will influence the organisation's ability to achieve the benefits of the change. The process of making detailed plans for change should include a search for possible second-order effects that could derail the desired impact:

- try to identify both the first-order and second-order effects of the planned changes

- be prepared for a continuous process of change and development as the first-order and second-order changes ripple through the organisation

- be aware of the need for continuing enhancement and upgrading of IT as additional requirements for change become apparent

- be prepared to recognise unintended consequences of change, including benefits that were not originally planned

- be prepared for experimentation and backtracking

- learn from the impacts of the change, and feed this learning forward to subsequent change efforts

- recognise that no design for change can be complete

- recognise that many people will think something is going to change, and will act accordingly – even if no change is planned; perceptions of change can be as influential as actual change.

The vision and strategy section set out the principle of change as a cycle of events. The lessons you learn in the later stages of the change process will be valuable for future change efforts – both in your organisation and possibly further afield.

7.3 The change owner

It is important to identify the single individual who will be responsible for the success of the change – the change owner. This may be you, your line manager, or a more senior figure in the organisation.

It is essential that the change owner has the necessary authority, visibility and credibility in the organisation to address the cultural and political obstacles to far-reaching change. The change owner ensures that the change process is focused, throughout its lifecycle, on delivering its objectives and the projected benefits. They must be recognised throughout the organisation as the owner of the change.

It is the change owner's job to make sure the business case is reviewed continually, and that any proposed amendments to the change process are checked for their effects on the business case.

Change owners also provide a point of unitary authority with which the project can be identified, avoiding the problems associated with committee-run projects and programmes. Authority is much more effective when it rests, and is seen to rest, with a single individual. One crucial authority held by the change owner is veto: the power to abandon or fundamentally redirect the change process if it becomes necessary.

The change owner will also be responsible for taking into account the views of different stakeholders in the change process and for overseeing the management of risk (see section 5.4).

Many examples have been seen in the public sector of major change efforts that failed, fell short or delivered late as a result of diffuse authority, whether perceived or actual. The selection and nomination of a single change owner will go a long way towards avoiding such problems.

7.4 The importance of management commitment

Without the commitment and direct involvement of senior management, a transformational change is unlikely to progress very far. Senior management are responsible for defining the direction of the business and establishing frameworks to achieve the desired objectives. They must make clear their support for the change – if people affected by the change see a lack of commitment on their part, credibility will be damaged. Key managers should be seen to be taking a personal interest in the progress and achievements of the change effort.

Management must take the lead in establishing the values and behaviours required by the change effort, and this may mean leading by example. For instance, if a change programme involves the introduction of new IT facilities in offices, the adoption of the new technology by senior managers will send a clear, positive message throughout the organisation.

A major change, and in particular the period of transition to the desired state, will be a time of uncertainty. Many of the normal operating procedures, reporting relationships and allocations of responsibility will no longer apply. Management must take the lead in establishing a style of leadership appropriate to the organisation and the nature of the change. In most change situations there will need to be increased emphasis on motivation of staff, promotion of teamworking, empowerment at all levels in the organisation, encouragement of initiatives and tolerance of risk-taking. Management must provide leadership in encouraging these changes in staff attitudes.

In a programme management environment, the group of senior managers who need to be committed to the change is known as the Sponsoring Group.

7.5 The business case

A business case is a document in which the reasons, advantages and justifications for a possible course of action are set out. It should demonstrate that the proposed approach is achievable, affordable and good value for money, both now and in the future. It is useful not only for focusing thought on the genuine reasons for change, but also as a way to demonstrate to senior management why the change process should proceed. During the development of the business case you are looking at these areas:

- is the proposed change affordable – that is, do we have the budget in principle?

- is it achievable – that is, can we make a realistic assessment of our ability to cope with the scale of change envisaged?

- is it likely to be value for money – that is, can we identify the most commercially attractive way of working with providers?

- have we explored all the options for achieving the change?

The business case for a process of change should include coverage of the following issues, which have been discussed in chapters 3, 4, 5 and 6:

- the drivers for change and stability that act upon your organisation

- what needs to change in your organisation

- where the organisation should be, possibly including an explicit change goal

- how ready the organisation is to change – more specifically in terms of its organisational structure, inter-organisational position, culture and IT infrastructure

- who the stakeholders are in the change, what they stand to gain or lose, and how they might be brought 'on board'

- how the proposed change is to be achieved – through transformational, incremental or modular change

- how the interim period will be handled, and what 'quick wins' (if any) can be produced in this period to generate enthusiasm for the change

- what the risks of change are, including the risks of not changing

- the cost of the change in relation to the benefits that will be gained.

For more detail on the business case and its development, see OGC guidance on the subject.

7.6	Change champions

The commitment of senior management to the change effort is essential, but it is not sufficient to ensure the success of the programme. In a 'pluralist' organisation there will inevitably be a multiplicity of views on the proposed change, and the way in which it should (or should not) be conducted. Part of the task of the change management team will be to identify the sources of support and resistance, and in particular to find those individuals who can be regarded as 'change champions': individuals who support the change and who are in a position to influence others.

A change champion does not necessarily hold a management position, but the individual has power within the organisation. The power may derive, for example, from their expertise, their ability to influence colleagues, their network of contacts throughout the organisation, or their understanding of its politics and personalities. Change champions can be used as members of task forces and focus groups, to generate ideas supporting the change, to promote enthusiasm for the change, to communicate the change message within the organisation, and to provide feedback on grass-roots reaction to the change message.

7.7 The change team

It will be easier to identify change champions if they are, or can become, key stakeholders in the success of the change. While support is welcome from any quarter, a powerful ally who has much to gain from the success of the change will be invaluable.

The staff responsible to the management for the planning and implementation of the change will need to incorporate a mix of skills. Depending on the magnitude of the change, the skills of the change team may include:

- programme and project management

- problem and conflict resolution

- business process analysis and re-engineering

- information collection and interpretation

- understanding of relevant IT issues

- knowledge of the business

- 'people skills': communication, persuasion, diplomacy, tact, patience and the ability and willingness to listen.

Additional skills may need to be brought in as required. Technical expertise will not be sufficient for an organisational change effort – the team will need to possess interpersonal and political skills, and a good understanding of the culture of the organisation. If the team is to be effective, it must include innovators and creative thinkers; staff who are wedded to the status quo are unlikely to generate the momentum required for pushing through the change.

It will be essential for the change team to have credibility within the organisation. The team members must be respected by management and staff for their sensitivity to the concerns of all parties, while being able to drive through the changes required.

The physical location of the team can be important. If the team is located remotely from the rest of the organisation, it may be regarded as isolated, out of touch and therefore irrelevant by members of staff.

7.8 Communication

Every organisational change effort will depend for its success on effective communications. Amid the fear, uncertainty and doubt engendered by a major change programme, there is scope for rumour, half-truths and untruths to flourish. Those closest to the change process must take the lead in communicating information on what will happen, what is happening, and what has happened – and the implications for the organisation.

The aims of the communication effort will be to:

- identify the people inside and outside the organisation who need to be kept informed about the change effort

- identify the key messages for the change effort, and the impact these will have on different parts of the organisation

- ensure that the reasons for the change, the objectives of the change programme, the benefits expected, and the approach to the change, are understood by all concerned

- identify the communications channels to be used and the types and frequency of messages to be issued for each category of recipient

- plan the mechanisms for two-way communication, and for receiving, recording and handling responses and feedback

- identify the roles of the change team, corporate management, change champions and other stakeholders in communications for the change effort.

An important element of the communications will be the means of advertising success: disseminating information on the 'quick wins' achieved in the change programme. Generating an atmosphere of progress will help to reduce resistance to the roll-out of the change.

It will be vital for the communications to be co-ordinated with the other activities in the change effort – the message must be consistent with the action. If there are conflicts between the messages being issued and evidence on the ground, the credibility of the change effort will be undermined. Communications must be timely, honest, relevant and trustworthy. Information must also be complete; any gaps will be filled by rumour and the output of the corporate grapevine.

7.9 Staff involvement

Staff will be more likely to accept the change if they have been involved in the planning and implementation processes. There must be opportunities to get staff involved in the decision-making; solicit opinions and ideas about problems or approaches. A suggested target is to get at least 10% of the affected workforce directly involved in decision-making for the change effort. Staff who have contributed their views in a constructive setting are more likely to endorse the rationale for the change. The staff concerned must be encouraged to take ownership of the change and become committed to it. Taking account of objections demonstrates flexibility; it also allows the change manager to identify objections and deal with them.

7.10 Staff development and training

During the transition period, at the cutover point for the change and in the early stages of implementation, all the staff involved must be adequately prepared and supported. The training and development of staff must be:

- tailored as required to the specific tasks and responsibilities of each category of staff

- reinforced as necessary with support facilities, counselling, refresher training and updates

- timed to match the timetable for implementation for each category of staff – training delivered too early will be forgotten and therefore wasted

- repeated as necessary for new staff and those transferred to different duties.

All staff must know the part they will be required to play in the change, and be fully prepared for it.

Staff training and development needs to go beyond the transfer of the mechanical skills required to operate new information systems or new administrative procedures. The opportunity should be taken to initiate the institutionalisation of the change – the 'refreezing' of behaviours and attitudes in the new desired configuration. Staff need to feel comfortable with the changes, and to feel confident in their abilities to work in new ways; otherwise they may revert to previous work habits and modes of operation. Plans must be made for support facilities such as helpdesks, support groups, documentation and online help facilities, and liaison officers to support individual workgroups. The staff who will need most help should be identified and special arrangements made for them.

The first weeks or months of actual operation following a change will be critical for those affected, and it is essential to provide responsive support facilities to deal with queries, problems and suggestions. Staff must not feel that they have been left to 'sink or swim' with the new arrangements, and allowance must be made for those who have genuine difficulty in accommodating the new arrangements. However, the organisation must demonstrate that there can be no return to the earlier state. For example, conformance with the new arrangements can be publicly recognised or rewarded, and failure to demonstrate the required change must be challenged. If it becomes clear that lack of conformance with the new arrangements goes unnoticed, then staff will naturally come to believe that the organisation is not serious about the change, and 'backsliding' will occur. An emphasis on staff training and development may itself represent a culture change for the organisation – but it is an essential element in the successful implementation of organisational change.

7.11 Overcoming resistance to change

In any organisational change effort some resistance is almost inevitable; in a 'pluralist' organisation it must be expected. Yet people are remarkably adaptable and willing to accept change – the changes that have taken place in the public sector over the last twenty years attest to its capacity to absorb change. However, it is to be expected that staff will resist change if they think it will leave them worse off in some way. Individuals are bound to ask what the change will mean for them personally, and arguments based on 'the good of the organisation' will carry less weight than personal considerations. If people broadly accept the status quo, they are likely to perceive the disadvantages of any change before they acknowledge the (perhaps less obvious) advantages. Resistance to change may arise from:

- **fear of the unknown**: people will resist change if they feel that it represents a 'leap in the dark'; the proposed course of action and the consequences need to be spelled out to those who will be affected

- **fear of failure**: the proposed changes may expose people to new tasks, practices, technology, etc, and they may be insecure and uncertain of their ability to handle the new situation

- **concern over changes to established practice**: people may worry that the change will overturn traditions which have become entrenched within the organisation and which form part of the organisational culture

- **lack of confidence in the change management**: staff in the organisation may not believe that the change programme is adequately managed; or that there is too much reliance on external support

- **lack of involvement**: for individuals, as for organisations, the 'not invented here' reaction can produce resistance to proposed changes; if people have been involved in planning and preparing for the change, they are more likely to accept it

- **objections to imposition of change**: if people feel that the change has been imposed without allowing them to express any opinion about it, they are unlikely to give it their support

- **misunderstandings**: people may simply have the wrong idea about what is intended

- **different perceptions of the change**: people may well understand what is intended by the change, but differ from senior management in their views of the desirability of the change

- **changes in power relationships**: organisational change is likely to be interpreted in terms of winners and losers; those who perceive that they will be losers are likely to oppose the change

- **corporate memory**: previous attempts at introducing change – perhaps the same type of change as the current programme – will influence people's attitudes towards the change programme.

The list could be extended almost indefinitely. There are many possible sources of resistance to change, and a critical task of the change programme will be to identify and anticipate resistance, and develop measures to address it – for example, though Force Field analysis as described in chapter 3.

There are many ways to deal with resistance to change. The importance of communication and involvement has already been stressed above: involving staff in decision-making is a way of getting their commitment to the decisions taken. Staff should be involved in information gathering and interpreting data that support the need for the change. Resistance can be handled by giving special consideration to staff who could obstruct the change – for example, by offering them key roles in the change organisation or in decision-making.

Table 3
Summary of strategies
for dealing with
resistance

Strategies for dealing with resistance are based on continuous two-way communication and involvement of staff

Approach	Commonly used in situations:	Advantages	Drawbacks
Education and communication	Where there is lack of information or inaccurate information and analysis.	Once persuaded, people will often help with the implementation of the change.	Can be very time-consuming if lots of people are involved.
Participation and involvement	Where the initiators do not have all the information they need to design the change, and where others have considerable power to resist.	People who participate will be committed to implementing change, and any relevant information they have will be integrated into the change plan.	Can be very time-consuming if participators design an inappropriate change.
Facilitation and support	Where people are resisting because of adjustment problems.	No other approach works as well with adjustment problems.	Can be time-consuming, expensive, and still fail.
Negotiation and agreement	Where someone or some group will clearly lose out in a change, and where that group has considerable power to resist.	Sometimes it is a relatively easy way to avoid major resistance.	Can be too expensive in many cases if it alerts others to negotiate for compliance.
Manipulation and co-option	Where other tactics will not work, or are too expensive.	It can be a relatively quick and inexpensive solution to resistance problems.	Can lead to future problems if people feel manipulated.
Explicit and implicit coercion	Where speed is essential, and the change initiators possess considerable power.	It is speedy, and can overcome any kind of resistance.	Can be risky if it leaves people angry with the initiators.

Other approaches to handling resistance are:

- **make trade-offs**: be prepared to cede something of value to members of the group in exchange for lessening resistance and making a commitment to the change. (This tactic may be most useful in dealing with external stakeholders)

- **work through the change champion**: use the power relationships and groupings in the organisation to favour the change. Ensure that the change is sponsored by one or more managers with high prestige and influence coupled with legitimate power and charisma

- **create group prestige**: enhance the attractiveness and desirability of a group to its members with respect to the beneficial changes which will be implemented, and its capacity to satisfy the needs of its members. Try to establish the reputation of the group as being at the 'cutting edge' of progress and achievement

- **retain links with the past**: do not assume that staff will automatically welcome the announcement of 'improvements' in procedures. Implicit or overt criticism of the past may be taken as criticism of the individuals who helped to create it, or who were happy with the status quo. If the climate for change is questionable, the change proposition may initially be presented as 'supporting' rather than 'displacing' current operations

- **retain familiar practices**: do not make changes arbitrarily; retain established workgroups and routines where possible, to reduce the impact of the change (but not where they would inhibit the introduction of the change). Change processes embedded in the immediate work situation tend to be more lasting

- **form coalitions**: work to establish agreements among parties who have common goals, where their combined strength and commitment will aid the change effort.

Pilot projects

Where there are doubts about the feasibility or outcome of the proposed change implementation, a pilot project may be used to investigate the issues and risks in more detail. Ideally the investigation will be conducted in a controlled environment, in which the effect of the factors under investigation can be isolated – but this will not always be possible. An example would be constructing a mock-up of new workplace arrangements to test new procedures using pilot versions of new systems.

The pilot project will enable the change team to assess what will and will not work in the change situation, and the advantages and disadvantages of different change actions. The results can be used to revise the change programme and reduce the inherent risks before going any further. It may be appropriate to use external experts or assessors in pilot projects to enhance the acceptability of the results.

Demonstration projects   A demonstration project may help to persuade doubters of the desirability of the proposed change; that it will work and will be acceptable. The demonstration project should replicate the expected conditions for live operation as far as possible, to add to the credibility of the results. Demonstrations conducted under easy, average and difficult conditions will test the robustness of the proposed solutions.

Although demonstrations are valuable, there are two situations in which they may not be appropriate, and the change team should aim to move directly to full implementation:

- where the opposition to the change is weak or fragmented, time spent on demonstration projects may be wasted, and full implementation could be the best approach

- where the opposition to the change is well-organised and strong, demonstration projects will give them targets to aim at; the recommended approach is to go straight for direct implementation – although it is acknowledged that this is a high-risk strategy if the opposition is very strong and determined.

In a situation where there are both technical and political difficulties, an appropriate approach would be to implement a pilot project to iron out the technical problems, followed by a demonstration project to win over the doubters. And in the absence of either type of difficulty, direct implementation could be attempted.

Realising the benefits

8

Your organisation initiated the change process to respond to issues confronting it and to achieve specific aims. You must review the programme to assess how successful you have been.

Review is an important part of the change process; do not allow your familiarity or weariness with the change programme make you omit it. It is vital that you find out whether the benefits you wanted from change are actually being brought about, and learn whatever you can from the process of change.

Obviously, learning lessons from change is likely to happen mainly after a change is complete. But lessons can be learned at any stage, and benefits should be managed carefully throughout the change process.

8.1 Benefits

A benefit is a positive outcome from change: changes are made to bring about benefits. But a change cannot produce benefits without active management. The identification, monitoring and measurement of benefits is fundamental to the change process. The various activities involved combine to form benefits management, an overarching technique that touches every stage of the change process.

Before a change, you will need to consider the benefits that will be obtained when the objectives have been achieved. Each benefit needs to be expressed in terms of where it will occur, who will benefit, who is responsible for its delivery, and how it will be measured. Monitoring, managing and reviewing benefits will form an important part of the review process.

Knowing what benefits will result from the change forms a key part of the cultural aspect of change, since people will want to know 'what's in it for them' or at least the organisation as a whole. Communicating the benefits may be vital if you need to overcome resistance to change.

The analysis and management of benefits is a fully developed technique that is treated more fully in the complementary guide *Managing Successful Programmes*. These notes provide an introduction.

Identifying benefits

You will need to identify and define your benefits so that you can monitor their progress. If benefits are not identified at the outset and individuals made accountable for their delivery, full realisation of benefits will never be achieved. To identify a benefit, you need to answer four questions:

- what exactly is this benefit?

- what differences (improvements for benefits, deficiencies for dis-benefits) will be noticeable after the change when this benefit comes 'on-stream'?

- where and when, in business terms, will this benefit arise?

- how will the benefit be quantified?

Many different types of benefit may result from change. The importance you attach to benefits will depend on what changes you are trying to make. Some examples of benefits are:

- **mandatory** (**must do**): benefits that allow an organisation to fulfil government policy objectives or satisfy legal requirements, where the organisation has no choice but to comply

- **improved economy**: doing what you do now cheaper, without compromising quality

- **improved efficiency**: doing more of what you do for the same cost, again without compromising quality

- **improved effectiveness**: doing things better – improving quality without having to compromise efficiency (do less) or economy (spend more money)

- **improved quality of service**: benefits to customers, such as quicker response to queries, providing more detailed, accurate information

- **internal management benefits**: benefits that are internal to the organisation, such as improving the quality of decision-making or management productivity

- **more motivated workforce**: the benefits of a better motivated workforce may lead on to a number of other benefits – for example, flexibility or increased productivity

- **risk reduction**: this might mean offering flexibility: keeping options open, or providing new ones, to prepare your organisation for an uncertain future

- **revenue enhancement and acceleration**: increasing revenue, or bringing in the same revenue quicker, or both

- **strategic fit**: enabling the benefits of other systems to be realised.

Benefits fall into three categories:

- those that can be both quantified and valued (direct financial benefits)

- those that can be quantified, but are difficult or impossible to value financially (direct non-financial benefits)

- those that can be identified, but cannot easily be quantified (indirect benefits).

Direct financial benefits that support your high-level strategies will be easier to justify than non-financial benefits, because they are of demonstrable value to your organisation.

Benefits will not necessarily represent a saving in cash terms. Some will be perceptions and impressions rather than specific tangible outcomes. It is important to recognise these intangible improvements and state how beneficial they can be. If your organisation is perceived – internally or externally – in a negative light, then a branding or corporate identity change would be highly beneficial, despite incurring considerable cost and providing no tangible benefit. In such cases, managing benefits may involve consultation with the public or market research to determine whether your change has been a success.

Some benefits may not come into effect until after the change has been completed for some time. Others may have been in effect from a relatively early stage – the 'quick wins' discussed in chapter 6.

Make sure that the modifications to business processes that are needed to enable each benefit are identified. This includes the changes in IT functionality that may be required to enable the changes you are proposing.

Dis-benefits

It is also important to consider the dis-benefits you expect from change. A dis-benefit is an unfavourable outcome of change. You may or may not have anticipated the dis-benefits of your change process.

An anticipated dis-benefit would be an inherent adverse consequence of the change process, such as increased workload for certain departments, reduced efficiency in the transition period, or worsening morale due to the demands of change. Although obviously not desirable in themselves, it may be that local or specific dis-benefits are unavoidable corollaries of benefits elsewhere in the organisation, or benefits that will be realised later.

Unanticipated dis-benefits become apparent during the change process and are normally due to problems at the implementation phase that were not foreseen when planning the change. An example would be disruption resulting from inadequate staff training.

Relating benefits to strategy

Your business strategy will help identify the types of benefit that should be achieved: the benefits you plan to derive from your change will be linked to the high-level objectives of your business strategy. Each one should represent a component of that strategy or a constructive step towards your change goal. If it does not, think carefully about whether the change process needs to be redirected slightly; benefits that are not linked to objectives may not actually be helpful to you.

It is important to distinguish between what you can do and what you should do; although a benefit may be easily achieved, it may not contribute to the 'big picture', serving only to distract you from strategic objectives. Spin-offs from core business areas, short-term sidelines and any other apparent 'quick wins' that seem to offer short-term gains outside your normal business area should be examined very carefully. Could your resources be better directed to doing more of what you do now – or just doing it better?

Dependent benefits

Some benefits depend on other benefits to be realised. Benefits that make other benefits possible are known as enabling benefits, or lower order benefits. Benefits that come about as a result of realising these benefits are known as higher order benefits. It may be that only the higher order benefits fit well with your overall strategy. Understanding the structure of benefits is vital in large-scale change programmes.

Lower order benefits are likely to be improvements or 'tweaks' that prepare the ground for other, more significant benefits. Clearly they will come on stream first and, if they do make a positive difference to the organisation, will represent the 'quick wins' that are a desirable product of modular or incremental change (see chapter 6). They are usually realised with the least management effort and are easily quantifiable.

Higher order benefits will be those that fit closely with your business strategy; realising them represents the achievement of one of your organisation's high-level business goals. However, this is likely to be at the price of greater effort, a longer timescale and preparation through achieving lower-level benefits first. An element of organisational complexity comes into play, since higher order benefits tend to spread out to affect different parts of the business; they could also spread out into other organisations.

Figure 7 shows an example benefits structure.

8.2 Evaluation and review in the public sector

All public sector organisations are under pressure to perform. Recent government initiatives have focused on the need for all public sector bodies to deliver greater efficiency, to ensure that the most effective results are obtained from available resources. Many change programmes in the public sector will continue to be concerned primarily with improving performance.

In many cases the organisation will have specific performance targets set, and programmes of radical change may be required to achieve those targets. In central government, for example, each department has drawn up a Public Service Agreement (PSA) which brings together information on aims and objectives, resources, performance and efficiency targets, and related policy objectives.

Programmes of change aimed at meeting performance targets will need to pay particular attention to the review phase and to the evaluation of outcomes of the programme. The organisation will be concerned to establish that the target performance levels have been achieved; but some thought should also be given to

Figure 7
Benefits structure

An example benefits structure, with lower order benefits providing the foundation for more general, higher order benefits

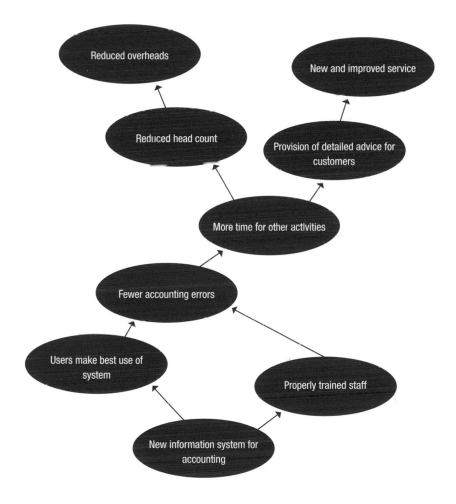

establishing the role of the change programme in meeting the objectives.
In complex programmes of organisational change, it can be difficult or even
impossible to establish, after the event, that specific activities or policies in the
change programme gave rise to identifiable and quantifiable improvements.
Chains of cause and effect must be carefully considered in planning the change,
and monitored during implementation. The approach to measurement of
performance improvements and other benefits must be considered as part of the
planning of the change programme, and not tacked on later as an afterthought.
Further guidance on performance management is given in the companion guide
How to manage Performance.

Roles and responsibilities

9

The key roles involved in a change initiative are:

- the change owner

- the stakeholders in the change

- the team responsible for bringing about the change.

This chapter outlines the responsibilities for the major roles, together with a summary of the skills and experience they will need. Some team roles may require full-time staffing throughout the life of the change initiative. The effort required for other roles might be consistent at less than full time contribution, or might fluctuate dependent on what is happening in the programme of change. Invariably, the team will combine people who are working full-time on the change with others who divide their time between the change effort and other duties.

9.1 The change owner

Overall responsibility, leadership and authority for the change is assigned to the role of change owner. If the change is large enough to merit the creation of a Sponsoring Group – a group of senior managers responsible for the business areas targeted by the change – the change owner will typically be one of this group.

The appointed change owner may only be involved part-time, but they must be visibly and consistently the driving force. The change owner is ultimately accountable for the success of the change and the individual appointed must have the authority to direct it effectively.

The change owner has personal accountability for realising the benefits and is responsible for:

- 'owning' the vision for the change

- overall control of implementation, with personal responsibility for achievement of the change (this should be an important measure of the change owner's performance as an individual)

- securing the investment required to 'make it happen' and realise the benefits

- establishing the change initiative, securing sufficient team resources and monitoring progress

- managing the interfaces and communication with stakeholders (see section 5.3)

- ensuring that the organisation and staff are managed carefully through the process of change from the old operational business environment to the new, that the results are reviewed, and that adjustments are made, if necessary, to achieve the results as planned

- ensuring alignment with the organisation's strategic direction

- ensuring that the aims of the change – and if it consists of a large programme, those of its constituent projects – continue to be aligned with evolving business needs

- commissioning reviews that formally assess the achievements of the project(s) and the benefits realised from the investment.

Successful change requires strong leadership and decision-making skills. However, different types of change require different types of leadership. The change owner needs to be able to combine realism with openness and clarity of expression to communicate a vision effectively. In addition, they must have:

- the strength to make decisions that are often strategic in nature

- access to and understanding of the business information necessary to make the right decisions

- access to, and stature with, key stakeholders

- the ability to communicate the aims and objectives of the change, and visibly to lead its execution.

9.2 The stakeholders

The stakeholders in a change will be varied, ranging from those who are expected to play an active part in making the change happen to those whose role is largely passive but whose commitment is still important because of the power they have to impede or resist the change. Some stakeholders are bodies or organisations; others are individuals.

Some important stakeholder responsibilities are listed below.

Senior management

The role of senior management as a key stakeholder group is to ensure that the change initiative contributes to the organisation's business strategy. They must be committed to the change and retain that commitment throughout the life of the change. They must lead by example and proactively foster enthusiasm for the change.

Strategic partners

Strategic partners could be service providers with whom you have a long-term partnering arrangement or they could be other organisations with whom you collaborate to provide an integrated service to customers. If their active participation and support is essential to the success of the change initiative, you should involve them from the earliest stages of planning. You should ensure that you have the buy-in of their senior management, perhaps through attendance at board meetings or equivalent strategic planning events.

Service providers

Depending on the level of support you will need from service providers, you should involve them at appropriate stages in the planning process. As a minimum, you should ensure that you have shared understanding of the implications of the change and how risks will be managed. In particular, you will need them to:

- be prepared to accept new ways of working

- react flexibly to changing needs within the organisation

- adapt to the particular demands of a transitional period.

Customers or the general public

Although this group may not be directly involved in shaping the change initiative, it is important to ensure that their requirements have been thoroughly investigated with consumer groups or their equivalent representatives. They must be informed of what the change means for them since they may need to obtain products or services in a new way to make a change initiative successful.

9.3 The team members

The roles of team members will vary depending on the change initiative, but will always include the following:

- a programme manager or equivalent team leader role

- a team member with detailed understanding of the business and its intended direction

- a team member with good technical understanding of what can or cannot be achieved with service providers

- a team member with responsibility for ensuring that the end-users' needs will be met.

The skills and competencies that will be required by the team managing a change will include the following:

- planning and scheduling

- budgeting and financial management

- quality assurance and quality review

- communication and interpersonal skills

- business analysis

- organisational behaviour analysis skills

- business and process modelling

- marketing

- project management

- programme management

- configuration management and change control

- leadership and people management

- report writing and information presentation

- negotiating skills

- risk analysis and management.

Recent experience of major change initiatives has shown that a realistic understanding of your team's capabilities is a major factor for success; conversely, where skills and experience have not been considered the risks of failure are high. You are strongly advised to carry out a skills audit of your team before the change initiative gets under way and monitor the skills profile throughout the change initiative (because real life situations dictate that team members often have to be deployed elsewhere). This will help you to identify any areas of weakness and make contingency plans to address them.

For more information on skills and competencies see the complementary guide *Managing Successful Programmes*.

9.4 Organisational learning

You should aim to ensure that the whole organisation benefits from lessons learned through the experience of implementing the change. Annex A provides a checklist of questions you should ask about the way your organisation manages its change initiatives.

There should be a role within the organisation responsible for carrying out reviews to assess how well change was managed, to identify recommendations for better approaches and to put those recommendations into practice. In this way your organisation should be able to make good use of lessons learned and to achieve ongoing improvements in the way it manages change in the future.

Annexes

Checklist – how well does your organisation manage change?

A

Positioning questions

The purpose of implementing plans is to deliver benefits for the business through effective management of change.

High-level questions

The high-level questions in this annex address key factors for success:

- Has your organisation translated high-level business plans into co-ordinated programmes in order to deliver business change?

- Are mechanisms in place that ensure that all projects are driven by business cases and that projects remain viable?

- Have good communication channels been provided internally, and do key stakeholders include providers of business solutions?

- Has a consistent structured approach towards programme and project management been adopted?

- Can you ensure that individuals have explicit roles and responsibilities within the change programme, with top management responsibility assigned to a change owner?

- Are plans in place for successful implementation that are agreed between customer and provider?

- Are you ensuring that new ways of working are successfully implemented?

- Has end-to-end management of risk been provided for throughout the process of business change?

- Has a detailed validation of business needs in relation to strategies and high-level business plans been carried out?

- Can you be sure that the proposed solutions for business change do not compromise strategic intent?

- Can you be sure that the required outcomes are both achievable and affordable?

- Have you set performance measures that relate directly to required business outcomes?

- Has a business-wide perspective in the management of risk throughout the change process been taken?

- Is information about risks collected and maintained (for example, through a risk register) that facilitates their monitoring and ensures that management remains effective?

- Have you made risk management an integral part of programmes and project management?

- Are the risks associated with radical change balanced against the benefits of business change?

- Do you understand the specific business environment, the organisation and its culture that will be affected by the change?

- Has the organisational capability and readiness to respond to change been appreciated?

- Does your organisation encourage innovative thinking about business options within the organisation and from solution providers?

- Is there any provision and maintenance of management information for monitoring and controlling change?

- Does any analysis of the potential impact of change on the organisation include the effects on partners and collaborators?

- Have steps been taken to ensure that the overall accountability for change rests with an appropriate individual (a change owner)?

- Have you ensured that management of change addresses business change as a whole, not just the IT components?

- Is there a benefits management regime in place for IT-related business change?

Detailed assessment   The purpose of this assessment is to show:

- critical factors for success (first column on the table overleaf)

- questions to probe to what extent these factors are present

- the extent to which the answers to the questions can be demonstrated – not at all, partly in place, largely in place, fully in place

- comments, issues etc as appropriate to individual assessments.

Contributory factor	Question	Extent (N P L F)	General comments, problems, issues and limiting factors
1. Good leadership	a. To what extent has the strategic direction of the organisation been adequately disseminated?		
	b. To what extent has the organisation culture been appraised, in terms of its readiness and willingness to accept change?		
	c. Is there a realistic view of the organisation's ability to cope with change?		
2. Defined responsibilities	a. To what extent does the overall accountability for change rest with an appropriate individual?		
	b. Does the organisation have access to appropriate individuals to enact programme and project management roles?		
	c. Is there a change owner for the overall change programme?		

Contributory factor	Question	Extent (N P L F)	General comments, problems, issues and limiting factors
3. Focus on the whole business change	a. Do you focus on the whole business change rather than just the IT components?		
	b. Are changes monitored adequately, e.g. the effect on various parts of the business?		
	c. Are the interdependencies between the business environment, staff and technology managed adequately?		
4. Robust risk management	a. Do you take a business-wide view of risk, rather than a project view?		
	b. Do you manage the risks inherent in change effectively?		
	c. Are supplier risks assessed adequately?		

Contributory factor	Question	Extent (N P L F)	General comments, problems, issues and limiting factors
5. Effective measurement and benefits management	a. To what extent do you assure that the systems and services delivered meet business needs and achieve value for money?		
	b. Do you measure the effectiveness of change programmes, e.g. in achieving business benefit?		
6. Good communication pathways	a. To what extent has the organisation established good relationships with service providers?		
	b. Are all levels of the organisation fully briefed on change plans and implications e.g. how their role is affected?		
	c. Do you know what others are doing that could affect your plans?		

Overview of Programme Management

Introduction

Programme Management is a structured framework for defining and implementing change within an organisation. The framework covers organisation, processes, outputs and ways of thinking that focus on delivering new capabilities and realising benefits from these capabilities. The new capabilities may be services, service improvements, working practices or products that are developed and delivered by projects. The programme selects or commissions projects, providing the overall co-ordination, control and integration of the projects' delivery.

Programme Management includes the process of managing benefits from their initial identification and definition through to the eventual realisation and achievement of measurable improvements. The driver for a programme is the ongoing viability and relevance of the programme's Business Case and the justification of benefit against costs.

The Programme Management environment

Figure 8 shows a typical environment for Programme Management. Business strategies are shaped by influences from both the internal and the external business environment. Programmes then need to be established to implement those strategies and also to implement further initiatives along the way. Even as programmes are in the process of implementing improvements to their target business operations, they may need to respond to changes in the strategies or to accommodate new initiatives.

Programmes, in turn, initiate or adopt the projects that are needed to create new products or service capabilities, or to effect changes in the business operations, until, finally, the vision for the future is achieved and the full benefits of the programme can be realised. A key element of managing a programme is to formulate a clear model of the improved business operations (this can be thought of as a Blueprint for those operations), which must be maintained and managed throughout the course of the programme.

Programme Management requires the understanding and management of:

- **benefits**: the identification and definition of benefits to the organisation and the management and measurement processes required to ensure that they are realised

- **risks and issues**: the recognition and management of risks that, if they happen, will adversely affect the operation of the programme and its outputs. Issues are current problems and challenges that require management intervention to enable the programme to remain on track

- **finance**: the financial management of all programme and project activities

- **stakeholders**: the identification of stakeholders, together with detailed analysis of their individual interests and involvement in the programme and its outcomes

- **communication**: the ongoing communication that establishes two-way information flows between the programme and its stakeholders

- **quality**: the process of building quality into the management of the programme and its deliverables

- **configuration management**: the control of documentation and key deliverables for the programme

- **process**: the management processes that identify and define the programme; establish the programme's infrastructure and plans; manage the projects and their delivery; and realise the benefits.

Figure 8 The Programme Management environment	The Programme Management environment, in which programmes are established to implement strategies and initiatives

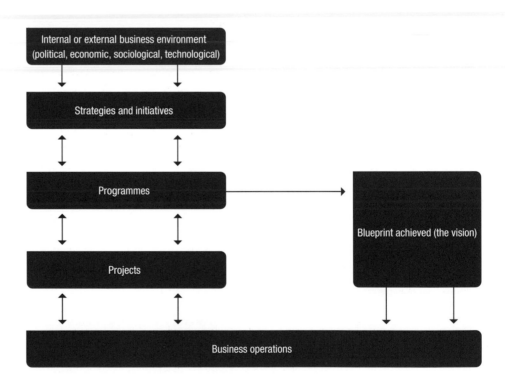

The Vision Statement

The Vision Statement is a customer-facing definition of what to expect from the transformed organisation, its service levels, cost, etc. The Vision Statement is used to communicate the 'end-goal' of the programme to the stakeholders. The new capability might be to deliver a particular service, to perform the same service but in a more efficient way, or simply to be better than the competition.

The Blueprint

The Blueprint defines the structure and composition of the changed organisation that, after delivery, should demonstrate the capabilities expressed in the Vision Statement. The Blueprint is a detailed description of what the organisation looks like in terms of its business processes, people, information systems and facilities and its data. It is used to maintain the focus of the programme on the delivery of the new capability.

Programme Management processes

The processes of Programme Management are:

- **identifying a programme**: to structure and formalise the programme based on the strategic initiatives of the sponsoring organisations

- **defining a programme**: to develop a complete definition of the programme such that the funding requirements can be committed

- **establishing a programme**: to set up the programme environment in terms of personnel, working practices and standards

- **managing the portfolio**: to manage the Project Portfolio such that the required benefits are delivered

- **delivering benefits**: to manage the benefits realisation process and to provide a transition to the new ways of working

- **closing a programme**: to formally close down the programme and confirm delivery of the Blueprint and Vision Statement.

Programme Management organisation

A Programme Management organisation structure, with clearly defined roles and responsibilities, is required in order to establish and define a programme and then effectively manage its implementation, delivery and realisation of benefits. The ultimate responsibility and accountability for the programme lies with the Programme Director who is drawn from the senior executives of the sponsoring organisation for the programme.

The Programme Manager is responsible for the setting up and running of the programme and co-ordinating the projects within it such that the required project outputs are delivered efficiently and effectively. The Business Change Manager is responsible for the benefits management process and ensuring the organisation is ready to take on the new capabilities delivered by the projects. The Business Change Manager ensures that the organisation is able to realise the benefits from the new capabilities.

There is a fundamental difference between the delivery of the new capability and actually realising measurable benefits as a result of implementing that capability. This difference is reflected in the complementary roles of Programme Manager and Business Change Manager.

Programme Management provides an umbrella under which several projects can be co-ordinated. This does not replace Project Management; rather, it is a supplementary framework (see Figure 8). Programmes need to be underpinned by a controlled environment of effective Project Management and reporting disciplines for all projects within the programme.

Further information

Relevant OGC publications

Companion IS Management and Business Change Guides:

- *How to manage Service Acquisition* (ISBN: 190309111X)

- *How to manage Service Provision* (ISBN: 1903091128)

- *How to manage Performance* (ISBN: 1903091136)

- *How to manage Business and IT Strategies* (ISBN: 1903091020)

- *Managing Partnerships* (ISBN: 1903091063)

Guidance on programme and project management:

- *Managing Successful Programmes* (ISBN: 0113300166)

- *Managing Successful Projects with PRINCE 2* (ISBN: 0113308558)

For more information about OGC's products and services, call the OGC Service Desk on 0845 000 4999 or visit the OGC website at www.ogc.gov.uk

Other publications

IT and Change – Research Project Report, ISRC-ITC-97017
J Ward and R Elvin
Information Systems Research Centre, Cranfield School of Management (1997)

Benefits Management – Best Practice Guidelines, ISRC-BM-97016
P Murray and J Ward
Information Systems Research Centre, Cranfield School of Management (1997)

Managing Change (2nd Edition)
Chris Mabey and Bill Mayon-White (eds)
Paul Chapman Publishing and Open University (1993); ISBN: 1 85396 226 0

Organizational Transitions (2nd Edition)
R Beckard and R T Harris
Addison-Wesley (1987); ISBN: 0 201 10887 9

Better Change: Best Practices for Transforming Your Organisation
Price Waterhouse Change Integration Team
McGraw Hill (1995); ISBN: 0 7863 0342 5

Effective Change
A Leigh and M Waters
Institute of Personnel and Development (1998); ISBN: 0 85292 741 X

Organisational change
Barbara Senior
Financial Times Management (1997); ISBN: 0 273 62491 1

IT and organizational transformation
R D Galliers & W R J Baets (eds)
Wiley (1998); ISBN: 0 471 97073 5

Steps to the Future – Fresh thinking on the management of IT-based organisational transformation
C Sauer, P W Yetton and Associates
Jossey Bass Publishers (1997); ISBN: 0 7879 0358 2

Information Management – the Organizational Dimension
M J Earl (ed)
OUP (1996); ISBN: 0 19 825760 0

The Corporation of the 1990s
M S Scott-Morton (ed)
OUP (1991); ISBN: 0 19 506358 9

Strategic Management for the Public Services
P Joyce
Open University Press (1999); ISBN: 0 335 20047 8

Strategic Planning for Public and Nonprofit organisations (revised edition)
J M Bryson
Jossey-Bass Publishers (1995); ISBN: 0 7879 0141 5

Organisational Behaviour
Fred Luthans
ISBN 0-07-113466-2

Index

How to manage Business Change